P9-AOL-329

CHARLES R. FRANK, JR.
with the assistance of Stephanie Levinson

Foreign Trade and Domestic Aid

THE BROOKINGS INSTITUTION
Washington, D.C.

THE BROOKINGS INSTITUTION
1775 Massachusetts Avenue, N.W., Washington, D.C. 20036

Library of Congress Cataloging in Publication Data:

Frank, Charles Raphael.
Foreign trade and domestic aid.
Includes bibliographical references and index.
1. Trade adjustment assistance—United States.
I. Levinson, Stephanie, joint author. II. Title.
HF1421.F7 382'.0973 76-51821
ISBN 0-8157-2914-6

1 2 3 4 5 6 7 8 9

THE BROOKINGS INSTITUTION is an independent organization devoted to nonpartisan research, education, and publication in economics, government, foreign policy, and the social sciences generally. Its principal purposes are to aid in the development of sound public policies and to promote public understanding of issues of national importance.

The Institution was founded on December 8, 1927, to merge the activities of the Institute for Government Research, founded in 1916, the Institute of Economics, founded in 1922, and the Robert Brookings Graduate School of Economics and Government, founded in 1924.

The Board of Trustees is responsible for the general administration of the Institution, while the immediate direction of the policies, program, and staff is vested in the President, assisted by an advisory committee of the officers and staff. The bylaws of the Institution state: "It is the function of the Trustees to make possible the conduct of scientific research, and publication, under the most favorable conditions, and to safeguard the independence of the research staff in the pursuit of their studies and in the publication of the results of such studies. It is not a part of their function to determine, control, or influence the conduct of particular investigations or the conclusions reached."

The President bears final responsibility for the decision to publish a manuscript as a Brookings book. In reaching his judgment on the competence, accuracy, and objectivity of each study, the President is advised by the director of the appropriate research program and weighs the views of a panel of expert outside readers who report to him in confidence on the quality of the work. Publication of a work signifies that it is deemed a competent treatment worthy of public consideration but does not imply endorsement of conclusions or recommendations.

The Institution maintains its position of neutrality on issues of public policy in order to safeguard the intellectual freedom of the staff. Hence interpretations or conclusions in Brookings publications should be understood to be solely those of the authors and should not be attributed to the Institution, to its trustees, officers, or other staff members, or to the organizations that support its research.

Foreword

THE Trade Expansion Act of 1962 and the Trade Act of 1974 that supplanted it were the first U.S. laws to authorize substantial aid to workers and firms adversely affected by competition from imports. This book analyzes experience under the 1962 act and evaluates the 1974 act in its light.

Mitigating the adverse consequences of import competition in the interest of securing the benefits of freer trade is not only a matter of international trade policy. It has an important bearing on labor and industrial policies as well. The author treats the subject in this broader context, emphasizing the public policy choice: should adjustment assistance be given only to offset losses from import competition, or should it—as the author concludes—be part of a national policy of assistance to workers, firms, and communities that suffer loss for that and other reasons? Accordingly, he proposes that various existing federal programs be adapted so as to help those disadvantaged by economic change however caused. He argues that the cost of such assistance is substantially less than the value of its benefits—in more efficient allocation of economic resources and hence improvement in the general welfare.

Charles R. Frank, Jr., who wrote this book as a Brookings senior fellow, became a member of the policy planning staff of the U.S. Department of State in 1974. He is indebted to Stephanie Levinson of the Brookings Foreign Policy Studies staff for drafting chapters 6–9 and for her research assistance throughout the project; to Peter Henle of the Congressional Research Service and William Diebold of the Council on Foreign Relations, whose comments on an early draft resulted in major improvements; and to Marvin Fooks of the U.S. Department of Labor and various other government officials for explaining the intricacies of the assistance programs administered by the Departments of Labor, Commerce, and Defense.

He is also grateful to his Brookings colleagues C. Fred Bergsten, Edward R. Fried, Andrew Gray, and Philip H. Trezise, who advised him on the design and execution of the analysis; to Deborah DuBourdieu and Randall Bolten for developing computational methods, carrying out the statistical analysis underlying chapter 2 and the appendixes, and verifying textual sources; to Claudette Simpson, Rosemary Taramino, and Ann Ziegler, who typed the manuscript in its many drafts; to Alice M. Carroll, who edited the book; and to Florence Robinson, who prepared the index.

The project was financially supported by the Rockefeller Foundation Visiting Professorship Program and by the U.S. Agency for International Development.

The views expressed here are the author's alone and should not be ascribed to the Rockefeller Foundation, the Agency for International Development, or any of those whose assistance is acknowledged above. Nor should they be attributed to the trustees, officers, or other staff members of the Brookings Institution.

GILBERT Y. STEINER
Acting President

January 1977
Washington, D.C.

Contents

1. Introduction 1

2. The Issues 7

Targets and Forms of Adjustment Assistance *8*
The Economic Security Rationale *10*
Encouraging Mobility of Resources *12*
The Compensation Principle *12*
Broad Approaches to Adjustment Assistance *21*

3. Import Competition and American Jobs 23

Output and Trade in Import-Competing Industries *23*
Factors Affecting the Growth of Employment *27*
Trade with Less Developed Countries *33*
Summary and Conclusions *36*

4. Early Experience with Adjustment Assistance 39

Assistance Provisions of the Trade Expansion Act of 1962 *40*
Action under the 1962 Act *45*
The Canadian-American Automotive Agreement *55*
Conclusions *57*

5. Assistance under the Trade Act of 1974 59

Eligibility Criteria *60*
Benefits for Workers and Firms *63*
The Older Worker *64*
Assistance for Communities *66*
Encouraging Workers to Move *67*
Early Warning and Timely Delivery of Benefits *68*
A Two-Tier System of Assistance *69*
Conclusions *70*

6. Aid to Communities and Regions 72

The Defense Department's Economic Adjustment Program *72*
The Studebaker Adjustment Program *79*
Aid to Depressed Regions *82*
Conclusions *88*

7. Helping Workers Adjust 90

Manpower Training *90*
Income Maintenance Programs *94*
Additional Security through Collective Bargaining *100*
Conclusions *108*

8. Industry Approaches to Adjustment 110

The Railroad Industry *110*
The Meat Packing Industry *115*
Conclusions *122*

9. Adjustment Assistance in Other Countries 124

The European Community *125*
Canada *129*
The United Kingdom *134*
The Federal Republic of Germany *139*
Sweden *141*
Japan *144*
Conclusions *146*

10. A Program for the Future 148

Trade Adjustment Assistance *148*
A Comprehensive Program of Assistance *150*
Conclusions *157*

Appendixes

A. The Cost of Adjustment Assistance Programs *158*
B. Statistical Data *170*

Index 174

Text Tables

3-1. Trade Ratios for Selected Import-Competing Industries, 1963, 1967, and 1971 25
3-2. Trade, Output, and Employment Data for Selected Import-Competing Industries, 1963, 1967, 1970, and 1971 26

3-3. Growth of Rates of Trade, Output, and Employment in Selected Import-Competing Industries, 1963–71 26
3-4. Sources of Growth of Employment in Selected Import-Competing Industries, 1963–71 29
3-5. Components of Growth in Employment in Selected Import-Competing Industries, 1963–71 30
3-6. Effect of Foreign Trade on Employment in Selected Import-Competing Industries, 1963–71 32
3-7. Annual Rates of Growth of Imports in Selected Import-Competing Industries in Less Developed Countries, 1964–71 34
3-8. Imports from Less Developed Countries as a Percentage of Total U.S. Output in Selected Import-Competing Industries, 1964 and 1971 35
3-9. Change in Number of Jobs Available Due to Increased Imports from Less Developed Countries in Selected Import-Competing Industries, 1964–71 37
4-1. Department of Commerce Action on Adjustment Assistance to Firms, December 1969 to April 2, 1975 50
4-2. Department of Commerce Authorizations for Trade Adjustment Assistance, through April 2, 1975 51
4-3. Adjustment Assistance Certifications by Department of Labor, October 1972 to April 2, 1975 54
6-1. Employment Attributable to Defense Expenditures, 1965 and 1968–76 74

Appendix Tables

A-1. Results of Regression Analysis of Import Competition in Selected U.S. Industries, 1963, 1967, 1970, and 1971 162
A-2. Number of Workers Eligible for Adjustment Assistance under Various Projected Trade Conditions, 1973–80 168
A-3. Estimated Cost of Worker Readjustment Allowances under the Trade Act of 1974 168

CHAPTER ONE

Introduction

FROM 1934, with the passage of the Trade Agreements Act, until the middle sixties, U.S. trade policies moved the country toward increasingly liberal trade relations with other noncommunist countries. The Trade Expansion Act of 1962, the high point in the liberalization efforts, provided the authority for the Kennedy Round of tariff negotiations under the auspices of the General Agreement on Tariffs and Trade (GATT) in Geneva. It also contained an important legislative innovation: a program of adjustment assistance for workers and firms injured by or threatened with injury from import competition. The act provided for supplemental unemployment benefits, retraining and placement services, and relocation allowances for workers. And for eligible firms it offered loans or loan guarantees, technical assistance, and tax relief.

The 1962 act, however, never fulfilled its promise for victims of liberalized trade. By 1970 neither organized labor nor the business community had reason to applaud the adjustment assistance program. At the height of the contest over U.S. trade policy in the early seventies the program seemed slated to die. Ultimately it not only survived but was strengthened in the Trade Act of 1974. That legislation affords an interested administration a means of offsetting the undesirable consequences of a liberal U.S. trade program.

Before the 1962 Trade Expansion Act was passed, the only help available to firms and workers injured by import competition was "escape clause" relief—either increased tariff protection or quantitative restrictions on imports of items that compete with those produced by the injured firms or workers. These clauses in bilateral or multilateral tariff agreements provide a means of escaping from injuries to particular firms and workers in one of the participating countries.

Escape clauses became an established part of the U.S. trade agreements program with a 1947 executive order by President Truman. The escape clause concept was later codified in the Trade Agreements Act of 1951. The principle is endorsed in article 19 of the General Agreement on Tariffs and Trade.[1]

Discontent with escape clause action led to increasing pressure in the fifties for some other form of relief for industries affected adversely by imports. The escape clause approach has three main defects, in Metzger's view.[2] First, its undesirable economic and foreign policy consequences inhibit use of the clause by the President. Between 1947 and 1962 the Tariff Commission referred a total of forty-one escape clause cases to the President. He refused to invoke the escape clause provisions in twenty-six of these cases, most often because of strong protests from abroad and concern over the deleterious economic effects on U.S. allies. Second, the escape clause is a mechanism for industrywide relief, even though the appropriate remedy may be assistance only to those few firms and workers most adversely affected and most in need of help in adjusting. Finally, the remedies it provides are not always the most appropriate forms of relief for the individual firms and workers in an adversely affected industry. Raising tariffs or imposing quotas will not guarantee that firms in an industry can raise the necessary capital to diversify or change lines of production. A worker may need help in retraining and assistance in moving. An import quota simply helps him stay a while longer at a job he may eventually have to leave anyway.

Unsatisfactory experience with the escape clause led to a number of proposals for an adjustment assistance program. Clair Wilcox, in a 1950 article considering various methods of assistance that had appeared in discussions of public policy, questioned the possibility of compensating victims of specific trade actions.[3] The Bell Report of 1953 suggested a

1. Stanley D. Metzger, "Adjustment Assistance," in U.S. Commission on International Trade and Investment Policy, *United States International Economic Policy in an Interdependent World,* vol. 1 (Government Printing Office, 1971), p. 320; known as the Williams Commission Report.

2. Ibid., pp. 322–23.

3. Clair Wilcox, "Relief for Victims of Tariff Cuts," *American Economic Review,* vol. 40 (December 1950), pp. 884–89.

number of devices to help industries affected by increased imports caused by tariff cuts.[4]

The most prominent proposal, that of David McDonald, president of the United Steelworkers of America, was published in the Randall Commission Report on foreign economic policy in 1954. The proposal called for extended unemployment compensation and retraining and relocation benefits for workers.[5] Later that year, bills proposing programs of adjustment assistance were introduced in both the House and the Senate. "Indeed, for the next eight years, adjustment assistance bills for workers were regularly dropped in the Congressional hopper, but no hearings were held on them, nor any serious consideration given them in the 1955 or 1958 trade agreement extension act deliberations in the Congress."[6]

Finally, in 1962 the Kennedy administration lent its support to the concept of trade adjustment assistance by including it in the proposed Trade Expansion Act. The adjustment assistance provisions of that act were crucial in enlisting the support of organized labor for its passage.

In 1965 the concept was again applied, this time to the automotive industry. In order to enlist the support of Walter Reuther and the United Automobile Workers for the passage of the Canadian-American Automotive Products Trade Act, the Johnson administration was obliged to include provisions for trade adjustment assistance. Under this act, the criteria for eligibility were liberalized and a special administrative body was created to simplify the application process.

The principle of adjustment assistance has never struck a particularly responsive chord with industry and trade interest groups. Industry's reluctance to embrace the concept stems in part from a fear of government interference in the affairs of private business. Furthermore, some of the largest and most powerful private enterprises producing import-competing goods have such a diversified production that competition from imports is not an important determinant of their profitability. The little help that the federal government might give them through adjustment assistance is not sufficient to make them strong supporters of the concept.

4. U.S. Public Advisory Board for Mutual Security, *A Trade and Tariff Policy in the National Interest* (GPO, 1953), pp. 66–67.

5. U.S. Commission on Foreign Economic Policy, *Report to the President and the Congress* (GPO, 1954), pp. 57–58.

6. Metzger, "Adjustment Assistance," p. 323.

Organized labor, however, has a primary interest in protecting workers' living standards. Adjustment assistance is a natural way to reconcile the goal of job stability with an often-conflicting goal of free trade. Liberal trade legislation was until the late sixties generally supported by labor, possibly because of a philosophical agreement with the concept of free trade and because it did not appear that import competition would have a significant effect on American employment. The enthusiasm that helped in the passage of the 1962 Trade Expansion Act, however, gradually turned to bitterness. From 1962 until 1969 not a single worker or firm received assistance. The eligibility criteria of the 1962 act were written very strictly, and a stern Tariff Commission ruled negatively on all but one petition for assistance. (In that one case, the commission recorded a tie vote, but the President did not authorize adjustment assistance.)

In the early seventies, a limited number of workers and firms did receive assistance. But the administrative machinery used in determining eligibility and dispensing benefits was so cumbersome that benefits were received only after unconscionably long delays. Little help was provided when it was needed, and even timely delivery could not compensate for what organized labor regarded as wholly inadequate benefit levels. Support by organized labor for adjustment assistance gradually changed to outright opposition. Adjustment assistance programs were attacked as "burial insurance" and as reflecting a cruel and deceptive attempt to buy labor's support for liberal trade policies.[7] The AFL-CIO's Industrial Union Department branded adjustment assistance "a flimflam. It does not and cannot meet the needs of those who are hurt by import competition. Furthermore, it does not meet—in fact it diverts attention from—the real issues, that is the maintenance of a strong economy and continuation of progressive social development."[8]

Along with the disillusionment over adjustment assistance came a change in labor sentiment toward liberal trade policies. Although some unions have always been protectionist, most of the major unions had tradi-

7. The opinions of some AFL-CIO leaders concerning trade adjustment assistance can be found in I. W. Abel, "Time For New Remedies," and in other articles in *Viewpoint,* vol. 1 (Summer 1971), pp. 1–3; and *Trade Adjustment Assistance,* hearings before the Subcommittee on Foreign Economic Policy of the House Committee on Foreign Affairs, 92:2 (GPO, 1972), pp. 37–119.

8. Stanley H. Ruttenberg and associates for the AFL-CIO, "Needed: A Constructive Foreign Trade Policy" (Washington: AFL-CIO, October 1971; processed), p. 110.

tionally supported liberal trade. However, some of them, such as the steelworkers union, abandoned their liberal trade position as early as 1965. The biggest shift began in 1969 with speeches by George Meany and other officials of the AFL-CIO. Organized labor supported the restrictive provisions of the 1970 trade legislation introduced by the House Ways and Means Committee and often referred to as the Mills bill. Labor opposition to liberal trade policies reached a climax in 1971 with publication of the AFL-CIO report "Needed: A Constructive Foreign Trade Policy" and its support of the highly restrictive Burke-Hartke bill introduced that year.[9]

Despite the general trend toward protectionism among organized labor, a few unions have continued to support liberal trade measures, the most notable of which is the UAW, representing automobile and aircraft workers. Some of these unions, while resenting the ineffectual nature of the adjustment assistance provisions of the 1962 Trade Expansion Act, pushed for restructuring the program. Many trade bills introduced in Congress in the early 1970s called for substantial improvements in adjustment assistance, the bills' supporters hoping thereby to gain broader labor support for liberal trade policies.

After extensive hearings in 1972 on adjustment assistance before Congressman John C. Culver's Subcommittee on Foreign Economic Policy of the House Committee on Foreign Affairs, it was expected that President Nixon would call for an improved program in his proposed trade legislation. However, the trade reform bill the administration introduced early in 1973 cut benefit levels sharply; of the new few proposals it contained regarding adjustment assistance most were designed to facilitate administration of the program.[10] Most of the benefits cut from the program were restored when the bill was passed by the House of Representatives late in 1974. The Senate Finance Committee further strengthened the program for firms and workers and added a new program of adjustment

9. For discussions of labor's role in the protectionist pressures of the late sixties and early seventies, see Irwin Ross, "Labor's Big Push for Protectionism," *Fortune*, March 1973, pp. 92 ff.; C. Fred Bergsten, "The Cost of Import Restrictions to American Consumers," in Robert E. Baldwin and J. David Richardson, eds., *International Trade and Finance* (Little, Brown, 1974), pp. 135–39; and C. Fred Bergsten, "Crisis in U.S. Trade Policy," *Foreign Affairs*, vol. 49 (July 1971), pp. 621–23.

10. See Charles R. Frank, Jr., *Adjustment Assistance: American Jobs and Trade with the Developing Countries*, development paper 13 (Washington: Overseas Development Council, June 1973), pp. 15–19.

assistance for communities. The bill was finally passed at the end of the year as the Trade Act of 1974.

Is a constructive program like that contained in the Trade Act of 1974 the best approach to trade adjustment assistance? Or should the United States try to facilitate economic change with a broader approach that emphasizes manpower policies, health and welfare measures, or regional and community development programs? Or does the federal government have no proper role in facilitating economic change, leaving the process of adjusting to economic dislocation entirely to market forces? These are the key policy questions that this study addresses.

The framework for analyzing the policy issues that arise in conjunction with adjustment assistance is set up in chapter 2. The magnitude of the adjustment problem in terms of job potential lost through foreign trade in import-competing industries is estimated in chapter 3. Chapters 4 through 9 are a series of case studies of trade adjustment assistance, adjustment assistance to regions and communities affected adversely by factors other than trade, broad assistance programs directed at individual workers, programs geared to problems in a particular industry, and adjustment assistance programs in other countries. The directions that public policy toward adjustment assistance might take in the future are assessed in chapter 10.

CHAPTER TWO

The Issues

ADJUSTMENT ASSISTANCE as a government policy tool can properly be viewed in a much broader context than trade alone. The American economy must adjust to rapid changes that are occurring in technology, in response to environmental concerns, and in reaction to critical shortages of minerals, fuels, food, and other basic commodities. Possibly government should assist in making adjustments needed in these areas as well as in those required as the result of government trade policy. The key issues discussed in this chapter that must be addressed by public policymakers concerned with economic adjustment are pertinent both to a specific program of trade adjustment assistance and to a broad approach to assistance.

The government's attitude toward assistance might vary from abstention to very active intervention. It is often argued that government should not actively intervene to facilitate any kind of economic change. Because labor and capital in the United States tend to be mobile, the progress of adjustment to economic dislocation is fairly rapid. Attempts by government to mitigate the adverse consequences of economic change may be costly and poorly administered and may actually slow down rather than speed up the process of change by providing financial support that enables labor and capital to remain in unviable lines of economic activity.

One view is that government programs should provide adjustment assistance for those affected by trade changes, but not necessarily general assistance. Such trade adjustment assistance can be used to provide a form of government insurance for firms and workers in industries subject to rapid and unpredictable changes in trade patterns; to facilitate the movement and efficient allocation of resources, and obtain the most from the international division of labor and comparative advantage; and to compensate the few who are injured by liberal trade policies, in order that much larger benefits can accrue to the general public.

Alternatively, a general approach to economic adjustment, regardless of the cause of dislocation, may be a more desirable policy. Many of the arguments for trade adjustment assistance can be applied equally well to government assistance in adjusting to other kinds of change. A program geared to trade invites a proliferation of specific programs that might be inconsistent and overlapping, cost more than a general aid program, and create serious inequities among workers and firms.

Only Canada and the United States have programs designed specifically to facilitate the movement of resources required by changes in trade patterns. However, recent bills introduced in the U.S. Congress have included special adjustment assistance provisions for firms and workers affected by the imposition of government standards of environmental quality and for those affected by the energy crisis.[1] Other countries, such as Sweden and Norway, have set up broad programs designed to help adjust labor supply and capital to economic dislocation, whatever its cause and in whatever sector of the economy it occurs.

Targets and Forms of Adjustment Assistance

If it is agreed that a program of adjustment assistance is desirable, then the appropriate targets of assistance and the form that assistance should take must be established. The targets may include individual workers, owners and managers of firms, industries as a whole, local communities that have suffered dislocation, or depressed regions.

Individual workers can be helped through manpower training and re-training programs and improved employment services such as counseling, testing, and job placement. In addition to helping workers to develop new skills or improve old ones and smoothing the transition from job to job, the government may help in maintaining their living standards during

1. See Peter Henle, "Worker Protection Provisions in Current Law and Proposed Legislation of the 93rd Congress" (Congressional Research Service, 1974; processed).

periods of unemployment, providing workers with income and with health insurance or pension rights while they are unemployed. Unemployment compensation, supplemental and unemployment benefits, social security, government health insurance, pension vesting, funding, and portability, food stamp programs, subsidized public housing, and rent supplements are the kinds of aid used in mitigating the consequences of job loss.

Assistance for firms can include technical aid, loans and loan guarantees, and tax credits and subsidies to scrap and replace inefficient equipment. Large firms might have less claim on this kind of assistance than small firms because it is the latter that usually face imperfect capital markets and do not have ready access to loans or other kinds of financing for modernizing and diversifying their investments.

Both workers and firms can be given aid if industries are the basic target of an assistance program. Such help might be accompanied by a government-sponsored rationalization plan for the industry. Most governments of industrialized countries have become involved at one time or another in reorganizing ailing industries or promoting new, technologically advanced industries. In Japan, for instance, government involvement is great. Although the federal government of the United States has tended to involve itself less in this manner, it has had a major role in reorganizing the railroad industry. The governments of England and Japan have intervened actively to rationalize their countries' textile industries. The French government has assisted in the development of a computer industry. The coal and steel industries in Europe were reorganized and adjustment assistance provided with the establishment of the European Coal and Steel Community. Canada and the United States attempted to rationalize production and trade in automobiles through the Canadian-American Automotive Agreement, offering adjustment assistance in both countries to facilitate implementation of the agreement.

Advocates of an industry approach to aid sometimes suggest that government involvement in industrial planning ought to be regularized, possibly by setting up an office of competitive assessment which could propose reorganization plans for declining industries.

Under a plan for communities or regions in need of special help, workers, firms, and local governments and authorities can benefit from an integrated aid package. Firms moving into the area might be given special tax advantages and subsidies. Local governments and authorities might be given technical assistance, grants, or loans and loan guarantees for roads, sewers, water supply, and other investments in infrastructure. In the awarding of federal government contracts, preference could be given to enterprises in target areas.

When an aid program focuses on a community or region, rather than on workers, firms usually are brought into the area, so that workers can stay put. The social and psychological costs of moving workers out of depressed regions to areas where jobs are available are great. Yet some communities may be so depressed that it is uneconomical for firms to locate there, given the need for proximity of supplies or markets, advanced social and economic infrastructure, or a source of skilled labor. These communities may have to offer very large subsidies to induce any reasonably large firm to locate there.

The target of an adjustment assistance program and the form it takes are issues independent of its overall scope. The rationale for a program that is foreign-trade oriented, however, is quite different from that of a program more general in its scope.

The Economic Security Rationale

Trade adjustment assistance can be viewed as an insurance scheme designed to protect vulnerable sectors of the economy from unforeseen changes in competitive position brought about by fluctuations in trade patterns. When imports increase dramatically or exports fall off sharply, firms may close or workers may be laid off. Even though new profitable opportunities may simultaneously be created in other industries whose export markets are expanding or whose import competition is slackening, workers and capital displaced by foreign competition do not automatically become reemployed in those industries.

The social costs of adjusting from one product line to another are often borne by those in the industries adversely affected by trade: workers lose their jobs and firms go out of business. Workers and capital employed in import- and export-competing industries are subject to a high degree of risk because foreign competition may cause demand for domestic output to fluctuate unpredictably.

Generally, firms are expected to bear the risks associated with entering their particular lines of business. They can diversify their range of products, selling some in relatively stable markets, in order to reduce risk. And workers who abhor uncertainty can seek jobs in less risky industries, although they may suffer some loss in pay in moving out of volatile industries since salaries are probably higher there to compensate for greater risk. Furthermore, workers may be able to protect themselves through collective bargaining from uncertainty over such matters as seniority, recall rights, and supplemental employment benefits.

The risk of losing a job, however, can never be eliminated completely. If it occurs, a worker might at best hope for reasonable compensation to maintain a decent living standard while temporarily out of work. Such insurance is unlikely to be provided by a private enterprise because of the threat of a general depression or even a severe recession, during which a private insurance fund would certainly go bankrupt. It is also doubtful that sufficient actuarial and statistical data exist for a firm to determine premiums for such insurance. Thus, only the federal government can provide unemployment compensation insurance.

Trade adjustment assistance might also be justified if fluctuations in economic activity caused by changing trade patterns are very large and unpredictable and have a substantial impact on the profitability of American firms and the welfare of workers. In many export- and import-competing industries, private and social risks diverge—the benefits to society brought about by increased productivity are offset by the private costs and risks to workers in shifting jobs and to owners of capital in shifting their investments from one line of production to another. To encourage an efficient flow of resources into those sectors that are vulnerable to foreign competition, special measures may have to be taken—for example, private market forces may have to be augmented by a government insurance scheme.

As instability in international trade increases, the case for trade adjustment assistance as insurance grows stronger. The growth in the speed of transport and communications has facilitated the proliferation of multinational corporations operating with little regard for international borders. Capital, technology, and high-level managerial skills can be transferred rapidly from country to country. Trade patterns, therefore, can shift much more quickly than ever before, causing more rapid dislocation among workers and small firms.

Encouraging Mobility of Resources

Trade adjustment assistance can be used to facilitate the movement of resources from sectors of the economy in which economic returns are low to sectors in which returns are high. Retraining programs and moving allowances can encourage workers to move into higher productivity jobs and more rapidly growing areas of the country. Loans and technical assistance for firms whose profits are affected adversely by import competition can enable them to shift their resources into more profitable lines of production.

Government policy may encourage labor to be less attached to specific jobs by providing for substantial income and fringe benefits during periods of unemployment. Such a program, if poorly designed, however, may be worse than no program at all in terms of efficient allocation of resources. For example, high unemployment benefits do not provide much stimulus to workers to find new employment. Thus, there may be a trade-off between ease of mobility and speed of mobility. While fewer workers may be encouraged to move if unemployment benefit levels are low, they may make the decision more rapidly than under a generous program. To provide substantial incentives to workers to find new jobs, unemployment programs might make benefit payments available in a lump sum or at a declining rate as the period of unemployment increases.

The Compensation Principle

Trade adjustment assistance is a natural application of the well-known principle of welfare economics that any government policy, presumed to be of net benefit to the nation as a whole, should not impose disproportionate costs on certain segments of the population. The government should offer compensation to those who might otherwise suffer from the imposition of its policies.

The concept of trade adjustment assistance as a form of compensation for those injured by liberal trade policies can be defended on a number of grounds. The significant benefits that liberal trade policies can bring to the general public far outweigh the costs to individual members or groups in a society. The individuals and groups within the United States who are likely to suffer from liberal trade are vulnerable on many other counts as well, and the opposition to liberal policies usually comes from these groups. Trade adjustment assistance is a sensible way of compensating those who suffer in order that the general public may benefit.

Gains from Liberal Trade Policies

Most of the general public will gain through the pursuit of more liberal trade policies. In particular, consumers gain and export industries and their workers gain. The costs of protectionist measures to the U.S. consumer are substantial. In 1971, Bergsten noted that "the total consumer cost of all . . . tariff and non-tariff restrictions cannot be quantified precisely. However, including the effects on competing domestic production, it clearly reaches $10 billion annually and may exceed $15 billion."[2] (Since then, the very high costs of quotas on meat and petroleum products included in his estimates have been removed.) Magee, using Bergsten's and other estimates of the cost of quantitative restrictions and his own more detailed estimate of the costs of tariffs, concluded that "the *total* costs to the United States of existing tariff and quota barriers to trade average $7.5 billion to $10.5 billion per year."[3] The cost of restrictions on textile imports alone, as estimated by Mintz, amounted to a minimum of $2.5 billion in 1972 and the cost of sugar quotas was $600 million in 1970 (the sugar quotas disappeared at the end of 1974).[4] Baldwin and Mutti's estimate of the costs of tariff restrictions alone (excluding quantitative restrictions) in textiles, chemicals, iron and steel, motor vehicles, and radio, television, and communications equipment added up to $1.15 billion in 1969.[5]

These estimates of the cost of trade restrictions are, in effect, estimates of the gross benefits that would accrue to consumers in the United States

2. C. Fred Bergsten, "The Cost of Import Restrictions to American Consumers," in Robert E. Baldwin and J. David Richardson, eds., *International Trade and Finance* (Little, Brown, 1974), p. 132.

3. Stephen P. Magee, "The Welfare Effects of Restrictions on U.S. Trade," *Brookings Papers on Economic Activity,* 3:1972, p. 701.

4. Ilse Mintz, *U.S. Import Quotas: Costs and Consequences* (American Enterprise Institute, 1973), pp. 59 and 43–44.

5. Robert Baldwin and John H. Mutti, "Policy Issues in Adjustment Assistance," in Helen Hughes, ed., *Prospects for Partnership: Industrialization and Trade Policies in the 1970s* (Johns Hopkins University Press for International Bank for Reconstruction and Development, 1973), p. 161.

if tariffs and restrictions on quantity were removed. They do not, however, take into account the transition costs that would be incurred by moving toward more liberal trade policies.[6] If tariffs were lowered and quotas removed, imports would begin to replace some domestic production. Some labor and capital might have to move out of the industries subjected to increased import competition. This labor and capital might be unemployed or underutilized for a period of time. The underutilization of labor and capital, the costs of moving and retraining workers, and the cost of adapting capital to new uses are real social costs that must be set off against the benefits of moving to a more liberal trade regime.

In an effort to measure these transition costs, Magee estimated that a five-year program of elimination of all U.S. restrictions on trade would cost about $330 million per year.[7] The adjustment costs of tariff removal in the five industries examined by Baldwin and Mutti would lie between $284 million and $578 million, compared to the gross benefit of $1.15 billion in 1969.[8]

Adjustment costs, of course, are transitory. Once labor and capital have shifted out of import-competing industries into more efficient industries, adjustment costs are no longer incurred. Gross benefits of more liberal trade, however, increase through time as the domestic markets expand. Thus the net benefits may be small at first but grow very large over the years; Magee, emphasizing this point,[9] took future benefits into account by discounting to obtain a present value. He estimated the present value of gross benefits to be $258 billion, and the present value of net benefits to be only slightly less (assuming that the transition costs would be $300 million over five years, or a total of $1.5 billion without any discounting).[10]

Bergsten has argued that unless the impetus to liberalize trade is maintained, protectionism will become the dominant force, resulting in a proliferation of trade barriers.[11] The benefits of avoiding new restrictions

6. For a discussion of transition costs and their effect on tariff levels, see John H. Cheh, "United States Concessions in the Kennedy Round and Short-Run Labor Adjustment Costs," *Journal of International Economics,* vol. 4 (November 1974), pp. 323–40.

7. Magee, "Welfare Effects of Restrictions," p. 682.

8. Baldwin and Mutti, "Policy Issues in Adjustment Assistance," p. 161.

9. Magee, "Welfare Effects of Restrictions," p. 686.

10. Ibid., pp. 701 and 699.

11. C. Fred Bergsten, "Future Directions for U.S. Trade," *American Journal of Agricultural Economics,* vol. 55 (May 1973), p. 280.

are just as important as the benefits of removing existing ones. Magee, for example, estimated that the cost of rolling U.S. imports for 1972 back to 1965–69 levels, as proposed in the Burke-Hartke bill, would have been $6.9 billion to $10.4 billion per year.[12]

Domestic groups are not the only beneficiaries of more liberal trade policies. Export interests in foreign countries also gain. In particular, the less developed countries have much to gain through relatively free access to U.S. markets.

The substantial economic benefits to both the United States and other countries are among many advantages that follow from the pursuit of more liberal trade policies. For example, Bergsten argues that a liberal import policy helps fight inflation.[13] More generally, the trade policy goals of the United States are inextricably linked to its overall foreign policy goals. A willingness to provide liberal access to U.S. markets may be the necessary quid pro quo in agreements on access to supplies of raw materials or energy supplies. Cooperation on matters of trade is often a concomitant of cooperation on monetary, financial, political, or national security matters.

Opposition to Liberal Trade

Despite the fact that the benefits to the public at large may be great, protectionist policies are often followed because of effective political pressure by interest groups who perceive that they are injured by liberal trade policies.

The political opposition to liberal trade reached a peak in the late sixties and very early seventies.[14] In 1964 Congress passed the Meat Import Act, and quite a number of attempts were made to negotiate voluntary export controls on textiles and steel. The Mills bill of 1970, a highly restrictionist measure, passed the House by a substantial majority, although it never was enacted into law. Protectionist sentiment reached a peak at about the time in 1971 that Senator Vance Hartke and Repre-

12. Magee, "Welfare Effects of Restrictions," p. 701.

13. Statement by C. Fred Bergsten, *The Trade Reform Act of 1973,* hearings before the Senate Committee on Finance, 93:2 (Government Printing Office, 1974), pt. 4, pp. 1624–30.

14. The development of the political opposition to liberal trade policies is described in C. Fred Bergsten, "Crisis in U.S. Trade Policy," *Foreign Affairs,* vol. 49 (July 1971), pp. 619–35.

sentative James Burke introduced their bill that would have rolled back 1972 imports to 1965–69 levels. Many supporters of this stringent legislation regarded it as an appropriate basis for future U.S. trade policy.

Support for protectionist measures decreased somewhat in 1972 and 1973 as the U.S. trade balance began to improve. Moreover, President Nixon offered a moderately liberal trade reform bill in 1973 which became even more liberal as it progressed through the House Ways and Means Committee and the Senate Finance Committee.

Part of the opposition to liberal trade policies comes from businessmen and trade and industry groups associated with industries that are under heavy pressure from imports. In recent years, however, the most significant opposition has come from organized labor. Even though the organized labor force as a whole might have a modest stake in liberal trade policies, a number of constituent unions of the AFL-CIO have had significant drops in membership that they attribute to the adverse impact of trade. For example, the electrical workers' union estimated that imports cost it 50,000 members during a five-year period over the late sixties and early seventies, the equivalent of almost a fifth of the union's total membership.[15] As Ross points out, "Every time a [union] member loses a permanent job, he loses seniority. Sometimes he loses pension rights as well. Thus a job loss numbered in the tens of thousands is enough to roil a union of several hundred thousand."[16]

Service industries and skill- and technology-intensive industries, whose workers tend to have an interest in maintaining export markets and liberal import policies, are relatively underrepresented in organized labor groups.[17] Bergsten argues that

> the AFL-CIO does not accurately represent the overall American labor force. Not only do its constituent unions represent less than 20 percent of all American workers; even this sample is highly skewed. Workers in the services industries (excluding contract construction, a special case) account for almost 70 percent of the total labor force, but only about 40 percent of the membership of the AFL-CIO. Traditional manufacturing industries, such as textiles and steel, make up almost three times as great a share of AFL-CIO membership as they do of the total labor force. Other proponents of protectionism, such as

15. Irwin Ross, "Labor's Big Push for Protectionism," *Fortune,* March 1973, p. 96.

16. Ibid., p. 95.

17. Lawrence Krause, "Trade Policy for the Seventies," *Columbia Journal of World Business,* vol. 6 (January–February 1971), pp. 7–10.

shoe and glass workers, are also over-represented. The high technology industries, such as chemicals and nonelectrical machinery, rely much more heavily on exports than most U.S. industries and are under-represented within the Federation.[18]

Organization of the service sector has been relatively difficult for union leaders. They view liberal trade policies as accelerating basic trends toward a service-oriented U.S. economy and thus as a threat to their political power.

Workers' high regard for job security may be another factor in union opposition to liberal trade policies. In a free and open economy, sharp changes in trade occur often and may cause rapid changes in employment in particular firms and industries. A structure of production geared to internal markets only and insulated from import competition would lessen the risk of workers losing their jobs. Even though a liberal trade regime might cause labor productivity to grow at a faster pace and real wages to increase more rapidly, workers may quite rationally reject these opportunities in return for more assurance of job stability and avoidance of the high costs associated with changing jobs and location.

Labor groups also may sense that a highly competitive and freely trading world economy has a tendency to reduce international differentials in wage levels. This notion is confirmed in the Heckscher-Ohlin trade model and in Samuelson and Stolper's use of that model to show the tendency for factor prices to be equalized among trading partners.[19] Since wages in the United States are relatively high, international equalization of wages poses the threat of a decline in the wage share of U.S. income and a retardation of increases in U.S. wages relative to countries whose wage rates are much lower.

The tendency toward wage equalization is less threatening to the extent that investments in human capital and advances in technology make U.S. labor more productive and highly skilled. Certainly this is a large part of the explanation for existing high wage levels in the United States. But the advantage of the U.S. worker becomes more precarious when viewed against the reductions in transportation and communications barriers, the rise of the multinational corporation, and the great increase in the mobility

18. Bergsten, "Cost of Import Restrictions," p. 135.

19. Paul A. Samuelson and Wolfgang F. Stolper, "Protection and Real Wages," *Review of Economic Studies,* vol. 9 (November 1941), pp. 58–73.

of capital and technology that have come about in the long period of relative peace and political stability among the world's largest and most powerful trading economies since World War II. The rapid movement of capital and technology, particularly to low-wage areas, hastens the movement toward equalized wages.

Labor groups quite correctly view the rise of the multinational corporation as the growth of an institution that facilitates the integration of labor markets by moving capital and technology to low-wage areas and, in the process, imparts labor skills in those areas through on-the-job training. Furthermore, multinational corporations integrate labor markets through the bargaining process, since they can always counter U.S. labor demands with the threat of further expansion overseas. The larger are the differences in wage rates between the United States and other countries, the more credible are such threats.

The support of organized labor for restrictions on trade may be more than just an attempt to protect vulnerable workers and industries from import competition. Rather, it may reflect a desire to insure that the U.S. economy is one vast protected market in which there is a reduced incentive to export capital and technology abroad to take advantage of low-cost labor, so that workers in import-competing industries can feel much more secure in their jobs. For example, under a protection scheme, firms that moved abroad might not be allowed to reenter U.S. markets because of import controls. Import controls would be only one aspect of a grand strategy, which might also include controls on or disincentives for U.S. investment abroad.

Trade Adjustment Assistance as the Solution

The political opposition to liberal trade is formidable and clearly justifiable for groups that are expected to bear a disproportionate share of the burden of adjustment. The political forces supporting liberal trade, on the other hand, tend to be weak and unorganized.

Protectionist policies are often followed because the potential losers from liberal trade policies are well organized and have a great deal of political influence. Organized labor is biased toward protectionism because of the nature of its membership and the structure of its organization. Consumer interests are not well organized, and foreign interest groups—particularly those from less developed countries—have virtually no say in determining U.S. trade policies.[20] And most important, the gains from liberal trade policies are widely dispersed and the costs are concentrated on a few. Those who stand to lose have much more at stake in trying to organize effective opposition to free trade policies than the gainers have in organizing support.

In principle, however, if total gains outweigh total losses, then those who gain ought to be able to compensate those who lose if a policy is implemented. Trade adjustment assistance can be viewed as providing the institutional mechanism for affecting that compensation in order to implement trade policy goals. Not only can adjustment assistance compensate those who bear the cost of freer trade policies, but its use can increase the commitment of those supporters of liberal trade policy who value the concept of fairness. Most people are reluctant to support programs that are of modest help to themselves but that would greatly injure others. In a nationwide survey of views on trade, for instance, respondents against freer trade most often objected that it would put American laborers out of work.[21] When asked, however, what their view would be if affected American workers were compensated and retrained, more than half of those respondents said their position would change from opposition to support of freer trade with the developing countries. (There was little discernible difference in the attitudes of union and nonunion households on these trade issues. In fact, respondents in union households were marginally more in favor of freer trade with the developing countries than those in nonunion households.)[22]

The program of trade adjustment assistance embodied in the 1962 Trade Expansion Act did not adequately serve to compensate those who had to bear the costs of liberal trade policies. The program included in the Trade Act of 1974 can do a far better job and might even stem the tide of organized labor opposition to liberal trade policies.[23] To some extent, adjustment assistance could alleviate labor's concern about unemployment, job insecurity, and the costs of job transition.

20. Multinational corporations based in the United States may, however, have both a significant interest in exporting from less developed countries and political influence in the United States.

21. See Paul A. Laudicina, *World Poverty and Development: A Survey of American Opinion,* monograph 8 (Washington: Overseas Development Council, 1973), pp. 51–57.

22. Ibid., p. 57.

23. The cost of such a program is estimated in appendix A.

Adjustment assistance, however, cannot completely alleviate labor's concern. Except for the training provisions, adjustment assistance does relatively little to redress the deterioration of labor's perceived bargaining position against multinational firms and the general tendency of returns of labor to move downward relative to returns to capital.

There are other ways in which these problems might be dealt with, such as full employment policies, broad manpower training programs, and measures for income redistribution. Losses in labor incomes from unemployment probably far outweigh the effect of any downward pressures on wages due to free trade and capital flows. Despite the increase in trade volume and the tendency of capital to move freely, the international equalization of wages probably occurs very slowly. Increasing workers' skills through training may raise labor incomes rapidly enough to offset these trends. Measures for income redistribution can offset the trend toward reduced labor income by enabling all income groups to have a share in the gains from trade.

Adjustment assistance cannot guarantee a worker a job that is like his last job in all respects. Working conditions might not be as good, the financial rewards and security not quite at the same level. More important, if a worker is emotionally attached to his job and his location, there is little likelihood that any reasonable financial reward in a new job will compensate him fully. There is an undertone in many of the arguments against free trade, even with adjustment assistance, that a man has an absolute right to keep his job. If this is the case, then adjustment assistance is not the appropriate remedy for job insecurity caused by changes in trade or by anything else. However, if the goal is to compensate a worker in the sense of providing a job that offers him an income and standard of living as good or maybe even better than before he was dislocated, then adjustment assistance may be an appropriate instrument.

Adjustment assistance cannot help the electrical workers' union to avoid losing members. Even with adjustment assistance, free trade will undermine traditional industrial unions and increase the importance of white-collar service unions. While it is impossible to gain the universal support of organized labor, some segments of the union movement may support liberal trade and trade adjustment assistance. Still other unions, basically uninterested in trade and neutral on the issue of trade adjustment assistance, might be convinced that a good trade adjustment assistance program would provide a precedent for attacking dislocations in their industries brought on by other factors. The general public is more likely to support liberal trade policies if they feel assured that affected workers will not suffer unduly.

Broad Approaches to Adjustment Assistance

A strong argument against a special program of trade adjustment assistance is that it diverts attention from the need for a broader approach that would provide assistance regardless of the cause of dislocation. Workers lose their jobs, firms lose money and go out of business, and industries decline for a variety of reasons:

Spending patterns change as incomes increase; old products lose their appeal, new products appear on the market.

Labor productivity increases so rapidly that higher levels of output are possible with a reduced work force.

Economies of scale and better technology in one industry change demand patterns for products of other industries.

Firms are badly run or their factories become obsolete; they fail and workers lose their jobs.

Changes in transport and technology require firms to move from one location to another.

Less expensive and higher quality imports replace domestically produced items.

Changing health, safety, and environmental standards require changes in products and increase costs.

Governmental budgets and procurement patterns change and shift demand from one industry to another.

Recessions reduce aggregate demand unevenly so that certain industries are hit particularly hard.

An overvalued currency reduces demand for some domestic products relative to foreign products, even those in which the United States has a comparative advantage.

All of these factors operate continuously in a dynamic, changing economy. All involve costs in the form of lost jobs, reductions in income, and reductions in the value of both financial and real assets for some segments of the population. All involve benefits in the form of increased income, job opportunities, and increases in the value of assets for other segments of the population. Therefore, it can be argued that adjustment assistance should be provided regardless of the source of the dislocation.

Or it might be argued that adjustment assistance should be provided only for those forms of dislocation that are caused by government policies. Defining what is meant by government policy is a problem, however. For injury can be held to arise as much from government's failure to act as from positive government action. The refusal to grant an airline route, to license a particular drug, or to grant a television license results in benefits to some but in injury to others. Thus, there is no objective basis to determine which dislocations are caused by government policy actions and which are not.

Whatever the arguments are in favor of a broad approach to adjustment assistance, prospects for a general program in the United States are not strong. Those prospects are most likely to brighten if government policies to compensate victims of trade dislocations prove effective.

CHAPTER THREE

Import Competition and American Jobs

ONE of the major concerns of those who oppose liberal trade policies is the effect of freer trade on employment. For example, the AFL-CIO claims that the rising tide of imports over the period 1966 to 1969 was responsible for a net loss of half a million jobs;[1] by 1971 this figure had risen to a total of 900,000.[2] The actual impact of imports and exports on production and employment in the import-competing manufacturing industries of the United States is analyzed in this chapter.

Output and Trade in Import-Competing Industries

Imports are either an important fraction of total output or important in absolute terms in one out of every five U.S. industries included in the five-digit level of the standard industrial classification (SIC).[3] These import-competing industries accounted for about 46 percent of total U.S. manufacturing output and 40 percent of total manufacturing employment in 1971.

1. Stanley H. Ruttenberg and associates for AFL-CIO, "Needed: A Constructive Foreign Trade Policy" (Washington: AFL-CIO, October 1971; processed), p. 62.

2. Irwin Ross, "Labor's Big Push for Protectionism," *Fortune,* March 1973, p. 95.

3. For a description of the SIC, see U.S. Office of Management and Budget, *Standard Industrial Classification Manual 1967.*

The analysis in this chapter is based on the 207 industries of the approximately 1,000 in the five-digit category in which, for at least one year between 1963 and 1969, imports were greater than 3 percent of domestic output and greater than $10 million, or were a significant fraction of output or very large in absolute value.[4] The five-digit level of classification is the finest breakdown for which it is possible to obtain output, employment, and value added data that match U.S. trade data.[5] Since it would be cumbersome to present information for 207 industries, they have been reaggregated to the two-digit level in the analysis. The two-digit sector aggregations represent only the import-competing five-digit industries selected for the analysis.

The variations in trade volume among industries were great, as table 3-1 indicates. In the sectors relating to chemicals, rubber and plastic products, machinery, electrical equipment, and transportation equipment, total imports by import-competing industries were substantially less than total exports in 1963. In most other sectors, imports exceeded exports, but the ratio of net imports (imports less exports) to output was less than 10 percent in all but the paper products sector. Gross imports were only 5.3 percent of output for all sectors combined, and since total exports exceeded total imports, the net import ratio was slightly negative.

By 1971, the gross import ratio had risen to 9.7 percent, and the net import ratio to 2.2 percent. In quite a number of five-digit import-competing industries, however, exports still exceeded imports in 1971. Even at the two-digit level of aggregation, exports substantially exceeded imports in the chemicals, machinery, and transportation equipment sectors.

While output in the import-competing industries grew quite rapidly between 1963 and 1971, employment was static, as tables 3-2 and 3-3 show. Total employees increased slightly, production workers grew hardly at all, and production man-hours declined slightly.

4. Industries that did not meet the 3 percent and $10 million criteria are included if imports were greater than 5 percent of output and exceeded $5 million, greater than 10 percent of output regardless of absolute value, or greater than $25 million regardless of the ratio of imports to output.

5. For this analysis, data on output (actually, shipments), employment, capital stock, and components of value added were matched against export and import data in a consistent fashion over time. See appendix B for a description of the sources and use of the data.

Table 3-1. *Trade Ratios for Selected Import-Competing Industries, 1963, 1967, and 1971*

Percentage of total output

	1963			*1967*			*1971*		
SIC industry class	*Imports*	*Exports*	*Net imports*	*Imports*	*Exports*	*Net imports*	*Imports*	*Exports*	*Net imports*
20. Processed foods	9.4	3.2	6.3	9.6	3.1	6.5	10.4	3.1	7.3
22. Textiles	10.2	2.6	7.6	9.2	2.4	6.8	10.6	3.0	7.6
23. Apparel	3.8	0.8	3.1	4.2	0.8	3.4	8.2	0.8	7.4
24. Wood products	10.7	2.5	8.2	11.0	3.1	7.9	13.9	3.2	10.7
25. Furniture	0.6	0.6	0.0	1.3	0.6	0.7	3.0	0.5	2.5
26. Paper products	85.9	17.9	68.1	88.2	18.0	70.2	98.1	22.0	76.0
27. Printing and publishing	1.2	0.4	0.8	2.2	0.6	1.6	7.9	0.6	7.3
28. Chemicals	2.9	9.5	−6.6	3.6	9.7	−6.1	6.1	10.5	−4.4
29. Petroleum and coal products	12.9	3.8	8.9	12.5	3.3	9.3	17.8	2.8	15.0
30. Rubber and plastic products	1.9	8.5	−6.6	3.3	3.9	−0.6	6.4	3.8	2.6
31. Leather products	5.0	1.5	3.5	8.2	1.4	6.8	17.1	1.4	15.7
32. Stone, clay, and glass products	9.1	5.4	3.7	9.9	5.9	4.1	11.3	6.6	4.6
33. Primary metal products	6.4	3.5	2.9	10.0	2.9	7.1	15.7	3.3	12.4
34. Fabricated metal products	2.9	4.2	−1.3	4.7	5.8	−1.2	6.9	7.1	−0.3
35. Machinery except electrical	3.8	19.3	−15.5	5.4	15.9	−10.5	8.2	19.5	−11.4
36. Electrical equipment and supplies	2.8	6.2	−3.4	5.1	6.3	−1.3	11.2	8.0	3.2
37. Transportation equipment	1.6	6.0	−4.4	5.1	7.7	−2.7	5.2	10.2	−5.3
38. Instruments	8.6	9.4	−0.8	8.2	9.4	−1.3	10.4	10.5	−0.1
39. Miscellaneous manufactures	6.7	3.8	3.0	9.0	4.4	4.6	13.5	5.5	8.1
Total	5.3	6.0	−0.7	7.0	6.2	0.8	9.7	7.5	2.2

Sources: Based on 207 industries in the five-digit standard industrial classification aggregated to the two-digit level. See appendix B for an explanation of the data used.

Table 3-2. *Trade, Output, and Employment Data for Selected Import-Competing Industries, 1963, 1967, 1970, and 1971*

Money amounts in billions of dollars

Item	*1963*[a]	*1967*	*1970*	*1971*
Output				
At current prices	194.86	253.56	286.09	307.25
At 1967 prices	204.42	253.56	260.76	270.50
Exports				
At current prices	12.38	15.73	22.38	22.88
At 1967 prices	13.03	15.73	20.46	20.18
Imports				
At current prices	10.08	17.63	27.82	29.78
At 1967 prices	10.64	17.63	25.33	26.10
Employees (millions)				
Total	7.86	8.71	8.29	8.29
Production	6.41	6.84	6.36	6.40

Sources: Same as table 3-1.
a. Data for 1963 are extrapolations based on the industry growth rates between the next year (1964, 1965, or 1966) for which data are available and 1967.

Table 3-3. *Growth of Rates of Trade, Output, and Employment in Selected Import-Competing Industries, 1963–71*

Percent per year

Item	*1963–67*[a]	*1967–70*	*1970–71*	*1963–71*[a]
Output				
At current prices	6.8	4.1	7.4	5.8
At 1967 prices	5.5	0.9	3.7	3.6
Exports				
At current prices	6.2	12.5	2.2	8.0
At 1967 prices	4.8	9.2	−1.4	5.6
Imports				
At current prices	15.0	16.4	7.0	14.5
At 1967 prices	13.5	12.9	3.0	11.9
Employees				
Total	2.6	−1.6	0.0	0.7
Production	1.6	−2.4	0.6	−0.0
Production man-hours	0.5	−2.8	0.0	−0.8

Sources: Same as table 3-1.
a. Data for 1963 are extrapolations of rates of growth between the next year for which data are available and 1967.

Factors Affecting the Growth of Employment

The lack of growth in employment can be attributed partly to the growth of imports. Clearly, however, other factors are involved. In order to analyze the impact of trade on employment, the change in employment can be broken down by increases in employment potential due to expansion of domestic demand D and exports X, and declines due to increased imports M and labor productivity P.

The growth of employment r_e in each of the five-digit, import-competing industries can be decomposed into these four components by using the following formula:[6]

$$r_e = r_d\,(D/Q) + r_x\,(X/Q) - r_m\,(M/Q) - r_p$$

where r_d, r_x, r_m, and r_p are the percentage rates of growth of domestic demand, exports, imports, and productivity, respectively. The ratios of domestic demand, exports, and imports, respectively, to output Q are the quotients D/Q, X/Q, and M/Q.[7] The terms $r_d\,(D/Q)$ and $r_x\,(X/Q)$ can

6. The derivation of this equation stems from two identities: abstracting from inventory changes, output Q is equal to domestic demand plus exports minus imports, or

$$Q = D + X - M, \tag{1}$$

and labor productivity is the ratio of output to employment E, or

$$P = Q/E. \tag{2}$$

When these identities are differentiated with respect to time T,

$$\left(\frac{1}{Q}\right)\left(\frac{dQ}{dT}\right) = \left(\frac{1}{D}\right)\left(\frac{dD}{dT}\right)\left(\frac{D}{Q}\right) + \left(\frac{1}{X}\right)\left(\frac{dX}{dT}\right)\left(\frac{X}{Q}\right) - \left(\frac{1}{M}\right)\left(\frac{dM}{dT}\right)\left(\frac{M}{Q}\right), \tag{3}$$

and

$$\left(\frac{1}{P}\right)\left(\frac{dP}{dT}\right) = \left(\frac{1}{Q}\right)\left(\frac{dQ}{dT}\right) - \left(\frac{1}{E}\right)\left(\frac{dE}{dt}\right). \tag{4}$$

Substituting equation 3 in equation 4 and solving the latter produces the equation for the rate of growth of employment.

7. Since the data cover discrete time periods rather than continuous time, it is impossible to calculate the instantaneous rates of change specified by the equation. Rather, rates of change are calculated on an annual percentage basis, which is then multiplied by the average of the beginning and terminal year ratios of domestic demand, exports, or imports to output. The rate—that is, the (negative) contribution—of productivity growth is calculated as a residual, by subtracting the contribu-

be interpreted as the contributions of the growth in domestic demand and exports, respectively, to the growth of employment, and r_m (M/Q) and r_p as the (negative) contributions of the growth of imports and productivity, respectively.

These terms reflect causal factors in the sense that if all but one of them were held constant, the percentage change in employment in the import-competing industry would be equal to the contribution of the variable factor. For example, the contribution of imports is the decline in employment that would result if output, exports, and productivity remained constant. Of course, changes in employment could be attributed to more basic causes that are not included in the formula—for example, to changes in prices or in tastes, and to changes in government monetary, fiscal, and exchange rate policies.

The contributing factors also fail to take into account indirect effects of changes in domestic demand, exports, and imports—that is, the changes that demand for products of a trade-affected industry will bring about in demand for products of the industries that supply it. Rather than being reflected in the trade contributions, these indirect demands are included in the concept of domestic demand used in the formula.

The decomposition of effects is based on real dollar values for output, exports, and imports and on total employees, production workers, and production man-hours. By far the most important factors affecting employment growth in the import-competing industries, as tables 3-4 and 3-5 indicate, are changes in domestic demand and labor productivity.[8] Increases in labor productivity had about six to nine times the negative impact that net foreign imports (imports less exports) had in the import-competing industries between 1963 and 1971. Growth in domestic demand had a favorable effect on employment equal to more than eight times the unfavorable effect of trade.

Table 3-4 indicates that, except for paper products, the effect of imports in percentage terms varied little across industries. The effect of imports on employment in the textile industry was relatively mild largely

---

tions of the other three factors from the employment growth rate. For some five-digit industries the rate of productivity growth calculated as a residual is substantially different from the rate calculated directly; at the two-digit level of aggregation, however, the error is quite small.

8. The contributions of the growth rates for production workers tend to lie between those for total employees and those for production man-hours.

Table 3-4. *Sources of Growth of Employment in Selected Import-Competing Industries, 1963–71*

Percent per year

SIC industry class	Growth rate		Contribution to growth of employment					
	Total employment[a] (1)	Production man-hours[b] (2)	Productivity per employee (3)	Productivity per man-hour (4)	Domestic demand (5)	Exports (6)	Imports (7)	Trade[c] (8)
20. Processed foods	0.5	0.2	2.7	−3.0	3.5	0.1	−0.4	−0.3
22. Textiles	−7.5	−7.7	−9.5	−9.7	2.2	0.1	−0.2	−0.1
23. Apparel	−3.6	−4.8	−6.2	−7.4	3.4	0.0	−0.8	−0.8
24. Wood products	0.9	0.7	−0.5	−0.8	1.9	0.1	−0.6	−0.5
25. Furniture	3.7	3.1	−0.6	−1.2	4.8	0.0	−0.5	−0.5
26. Paper products	0.3	−0.1	−3.1	−3.6	6.9	1.2	−4.7	−3.5
27. Printing and publishing	3.1	3.1	−0.4	−0.4	5.0	0.1	−1.5	−1.5
28. Chemicals	2.0	1.5	−2.9	−3.4	5.0	0.6	−0.7	−0.1
29. Petroleum and coal products	10.4	9.5	−5.4	4.6	6.4	0.0	−1.5	−1.5
30. Rubber and plastic products	4.2	3.8	−0.4	−0.8	7.0	−1.5	−1.0	−2.5
31. Leather products	−2.3	−2.7	−1.7	−2.1	1.2	0.0	−1.8	−1.8
32. Stone, clay, and glass products	1.2	0.6	−1.6	−2.2	3.0	0.3	−0.6	−0.2
33. Primary metal products	2.7	1.6	2.5	1.4	1.7	−0.1	−1.4	−1.5
34. Fabricated metal products	−0.4	−0.9	−3.4	−3.9	3.2	0.6	−0.8	−0.2
35. Machinery except electrical	2.4	0.3	−1.0	−3.1	3.6	0.7	−0.9	−0.2
36. Electrical equipment and supplies	2.8	−3.4	−2.8	−9.0	6.7	0.7	−1.8	−1.1
37. Transportation equipment	2.4	1.8	−1.9	−2.5	4.0	1.0	−0.7	0.3
38. Instruments	0.9	−1.4	−9.3	−11.6	10.3	1.2	−1.2	−0.1
39. Miscellaneous manufactures	0.8	−0.1	−2.4	−3.3	4.1	0.4	−1.3	−0.9
Total	0.7	−0.8	−2.9	−4.3	4.0	0.4	−0.9	−0.5

Sources: Same as table 3-1.

a. Algebraic sum of columns 3, 5, 6, and 7; numbers have been rounded.

b. Algebraic sum of columns 4, 5, 6, and 7; numbers have been rounded.

c. Algebraic sum of columns 6 and 7; numbers have been rounded.

Table 3-5. *Components of Growth in Employment in Selected Import-Competing Industries, 1963–71*

Percent per year

Years	*Growth rate of employment*	*Contribution of growth in*				
		Domestic demand	*Imports*	*Exports*	*Productivity*	*Net trade*
1963–67	2.6	6.0	−0.8	0.3	−2.9	−0.5
1967–70	−1.6	1.3	−1.1	0.6	−2.5	−0.4
1970–71	−0.0	4.2	−0.3	−0.1	−3.8	−0.4
1963–71	0.7	4.0	−0.9	0.4	−2.9	−0.5

Sources: Same as table 3-1.

because of the slow growth of cotton textile imports, which were inhibited by a quota system. Increased productivity, on the other hand, had an enormous impact on employment in textiles. Productivity in import-competing textiles increased at a rate of almost 10 percent, much more rapidly than in any other industry except instruments (where, because of the heterogeneity of output, productivity is of little value as a gauge). Another negative factor in the case of textiles was the rather sluggish growth of domestic demand. The importance of productivity increases in explaining the loss of jobs in the textile industry is corroborated in a careful statistical analysis by Peter Isard. He finds that new investment in the textile industry is concentrated on labor-saving devices and, furthermore, that much of the new investment is profitable only because the high tariffs and quantitative restrictions provide a high level of protection from imports.[9]

The United States is almost totally dependent on foreign sources of paper and paper products and hence the industry does not employ a large number of workers. In relative terms, however, the impact of imports on employment was particularly severe. Productivity growth was substantial, but despite the large negative effect of imports and productivity combined, total employment increased slightly, because of the rapid increase in domestic demand.

The sectors that showed the greatest percentage loss in job potential due to imports were paper, printing and publishing, petroleum and coal

9. "Employment Impact of Textile Imports and Investment: A Vintage Capital Model," *American Economic Review*, vol. 63 (June 1973), pp. 402–16.

products, leather products (mainly shoes), primary metal products (mainly steel), and electrical equipment and supplies (mainly radio and television receivers). Yet, of these, only the leather products sector suffered a decline in employment. The other sectors benefited either from rapid increases in domestic demand or very modest increases in productivity, so that employment growth was substantial despite the impact of imports.

Table 3-5 shows that the impact of imports was greatest over the period 1967 to 1970. Periods of increased imports, however, corresponded to periods of increased exports, so that the net contribution of trade remained relatively constant over time.

The effect of foreign trade in terms of absolute numbers of jobs lost is shown in table 3-6.[10] The net change in jobs varied considerably from year to year and industry to industry. Between 1963 and 1967 the net loss of jobs due to trade was about 151,500, or about 38,000 jobs a year. From 1967 to 1970 the net loss was about 119,200, or roughly 40,000 per year. Between 1970 and 1971 the loss was 83,200. Particularly volatile industries were those making primary metal (mostly steel) products and transportation equipment (mostly automobiles). Employment in the primary metals sector showed a net loss of about 9,000 per year from 1963 to 1967, a net gain of about 11,000 per year between 1967 and 1970, and a net loss of more than 68,000 jobs between 1970 and 1971. In the transportation equipment sector the net loss was about 5,000 per year from 1963 to 1967 and 14,000 a year between 1967 and 1970, with a net gain of almost 62,000 between 1970 and 1971. The total net loss of jobs between 1963 and 1971 was about 354,000 or roughly 44,000 jobs per year.

These figures do not include jobs lost indirectly because of reductions in sales by industries that supply the import-competing industries. If this factor were taken into account, the total number of jobs lost would be greater—by about one job lost indirectly for each direct loss of a job due to trade, according to Krause's estimate based on employment in manufacturing industries in 1971.[11] When applied to the roughly 44,000 jobs

10. The absolute job loss is determined by taking, for each two-digit industry, the ratio of the percentage change in employment due to imports and exports to the overall percentage change in employment, and multiplying that ratio by the absolute change in employment over the same period.

11. Lawrence B. Krause assisted by John A. Mathieson, "How Much of Current Unemployment Did We Import?" *Brookings Papers on Economic Activity,* 2:1971, p. 422.

Table 3-6. *Effect of Foreign Trade on Employment in Selected Import-Competing Industries, 1963–71*

Thousands of jobs[a]

SIC industry class	1963–67			1967–70			1970–71			1963–71		
	Exports	*Imports*	*Net imports*	*Exports*	*Imports*	*Net imports*	*Exports*	*Imports*	*Net imports*	*Exports*	*Imports*	*Net imports*
20. Processed foods	1.21	−5.11	−3.90	0.77	−6.86	−6.09	0.93	−1.00	−0.07	2.91	−12.97	−10.07
22. Textiles	0.67	−0.22	0.45	1.90	−2.19	−0.29	0.44	−3.17	−2.73	3.01	−5.58	−2.57
23. Apparel	2.23	−17.20	−14.97	−0.47	−24.68	−25.15	1.02	−15.94	−14.93	2.78	−57.83	−55.05
24. Wood products	2.44	−2.00	0.44	3.32	−5.79	−2.46	−1.56	−8.79	−10.35	4.20	−16.58	−12.38
25. Furniture	0.54	−3.64	−3.10	−0.24	−6.18	−6.41	−0.04	−2.77	−2.81	0.26	−12.58	−12.32
26. Paper products	1.04	−5.14	−4.10	5.12	−1.30	3.81	−2.06	−6.18	−8.25	4.10	−12.63	−8.53
27. Printing and publishing	0.04	−0.18	−0.13	0.00	−0.86	−0.86	−0.00	−0.03	−0.03	0.04	−1.07	−1.03
28. Chemicals	9.00	−6.00	3.00	12.08	−7.17	4.91	−2.24	−6.63	−8.86	18.84	−19.80	−0.96
29. Petroleum and coal products	0.13	−1.24	−1.11	1.05	−7.41	−6.36	−0.45	−1.48	−1.93	0.74	−10.14	−9.40
30. Rubber and plastic products	−32.27	−5.79	−38.06	1.30	−12.17	−10.87	1.33	−2.86	−1.53	−29.64	−20.82	−50.46
31. Leather products	0.23	−12.35	−12.11	−0.60	−19.38	−19.98	0.27	−3.40	−3.14	−0.10	−35.13	−35.23
32. Stone, clay, and glass products	2.24	−3.72	−1.49	1.65	−3.37	−1.72	−0.66	1.55	0.89	3.23	−5.54	−2.31
33. Primary metal products	−4.68	−30.96	−35.64	42.81	−9.39	33.42	−17.70	−50.36	−68.07	20.43	−90.72	−70.28
34. Fabricated metal products	7.05	−7.53	−0.48	3.44	−5.67	−2.23	0.16	−0.48	−0.32	10.65	−13.68	−3.03
35. Machinery except electrical	16.17	−23.43	−7.26	27.29	−14.94	12.35	−9.51	−3.80	−13.31	33.95	−42.17	−8.22
36. Electrical equipment and supplies	20.87	−30.15	−9.28	19.22	−55.04	−35.81	−1.15	−9.73	−10.88	38.95	−94.92	−55.97
37. Transportation equipment	43.55	−64.33	−20.79	39.88	−82.29	−42.41	19.43	42.42	61.85	102.85	−104.20	−1.35
38. Instruments	9.10	−7.39	1.71	4.60	−6.19	−1.59	1.16	−1.46	−0.30	14.86	−15.04	−0.17
39. Miscellaneous manufactures	3.25	−7.95	−4.71	1.10	−12.55	−11.45	2.70	−1.16	1.54	7.04	21.66	−14.62
Total	82.82	−234.34	−151.53	164.22	−283.42	−119.20	−7.93	−75.28	−83.22	239.10	−593.05	−353.94

Sources: Same as table 3-1.

a. Minus sign (−) indicates jobs lost.

lost directly, this ratio suggests a total of about 88,000 jobs lost per year due to trade in import-competing industries.

Since these figures apply to import-competing industries, they do not take into account job gains in industries that are principally engaged in exporting. The figures on job change for net foreign trade would be substantially more optimistic than those for the import-competing industries which this analysis is limited to.

Trade with Less Developed Countries

Much of the concern regarding the impact of import competition on U.S. jobs is directed at the growing imports of manufacturers from less developed countries (LDCs). As European and Japanese wage rates approach those of the United States, there seems to be a relaxation of concern that imports from these areas will undermine American jobs. Wage rates in less developed countries, however, are substantially below those in the United States. Of course, often productivity in those countries is also lower, so that lower wage rates do not necessarily imply the unfair advantage that is often assumed. Labor productivity in a particular industry, however, may be just as high in less developed countries as it is in the United States. Thus, U.S. workers in that industry might claim that LDC producers have an unfair advantage when, in fact, the industry's high worker productivity is simply a reflection of a comparative advantage in the less developed country.

Imports in import-competing industries grew more than twice as fast from less developed countries as from more advanced areas between 1964 and 1971—26.4 percent against 11.0 percent per annum (see table 3-7). In 1964, imports from less developed areas accounted for only 21 percent of total imports in import-competing industries, but by 1971 they had reached 40 percent, almost doubling in seven years. As table 3-7 indicates, however, Asian imports were largely responsible for this phenomenon, since imports from Latin American and African countries grew more slowly than all imports together.[12] Furthermore, even within Asia, the import growth was concentrated largely in four countries: Korea, Taiwan, Hong Kong, and Singapore.

12. In the early seventies, imports from Latin America to the United States grew much more rapidly than they did in the sixties.

Table 3-7. *Annual Rates of Growth of Imports in Selected Import-Competing Industries in Less Developed Countries, 1964–71*
Percent change in value of imports at current prices

SIC industry class	Less developed countries: Africa	Asia	Latin America	Total	Rest of world	Whole world
20. Processed foods	11.1	8.9	3.0	9.9	9.7	9.8
22. Textiles	1.6	8.9	12.1	8.0	−1.8	3.1
23. Apparel	58.7	35.4	−5.8	35.9	0.2	18.6
24. Wood products	10.6	22.8	−1.1	20.0	9.0	11.3
25. Furniture	27.8	48.0	0.0	43.4	27.9	30.4
26. Paper products	21.9	45.0	28.9	31.4	6.4	6.5
27. Printing and publishing	[a]	105.2	[a]	105.2	0.9	38.9
28. Chemicals	5.6	63.5	2.2	26.5	16.2	17.7
29. Petroleum and coal products	9.1	16.0	17.7	9.6	15.5	12.7
30. Rubber and plastic products	26.4	60.5	[a]	58.9	15.2	25.8
31. Leather products	32.7	26.8	25.8	28.5	18.4	20.4
32. Stone, clay, and glass products	11.7	65.8	[a]	46.8	2.1	7.8
33. Primary metal products	−1.6	45.3	5.8	20.5	15.2	16.7
34. Fabricated metal products	50.5	106.2	[a]	99.4	9.9	18.7
35. Machinery except electrical	75.4	168.5	[a]	138.2	16.2	20.1
36. Electrical equipment and supplies	128.3	90.9	−23.7	89.7	7.0	28.3
37. Transportation equipment	73.5	240.2	17.0	183.3	12.7	21.9
38. Instruments	36.9	110.8	[a]	108.9	5.9	14.1
39. Miscellaneous manufactures	45.3	31.8	[a]	32.5	2.4	14.7
Total	10.0	37.7	5.5	26.4	11.0	15.4

Sources: Same as table 3-1.
a. Imports were zero in 1964, so the rate of growth is infinite.

Nevertheless, as table 3-8 indicates, the penetration of LDC imports into the U.S. markets was substantial in a number of sectors. There were significant increases in imports from less developed countries, either in percentage or in absolute terms, in the apparel, printing and publishing, rubber and plastic products, fabricated metal products, electrical equipment and supplies, and instruments industries. In all sectors the ratio of imports from less developed countries to output more than tripled in the import-competing industries, while imports from all countries less than doubled as a percentage of U.S. output.

The increase in imports from less developed countries can also be translated into an impact on U.S. jobs. The changes in total imports from 1964 to 1971 from Africa, Asia, and Latin America are used to prorate

Table 3-8. *Imports from Less Developed Countries as a Percentage of Total U.S. Output in Selected Import-Competing Industries, 1964 and 1971*

	Less developed countries									
	Africa		*Asia*		*Latin America*		*Total*		*Whole world*	
SIC industry class	*1964*	*1971*	*1964*	*1971*	*1964*	*1971*	*1964*	*1971*	*1964*	*1971*
20. Processed foods	1.9	2.5	1.4	1.7	0.2	0.2	3.6	4.4	8.5	10.4
22. Textiles	0.7	0.7	3.5	5.4	0.1	0.2	4.3	6.3	9.9	10.6
23. Apparel	0.0	0.3	1.0	6.2	0.0	0.0	1.0	6.5	3.3	8.2
24. Wood products	0.3	0.5	1.2	3.4	0.1	0.1	1.7	3.9	10.1	13.9
25. Furniture	0.0	0.1	0.1	0.6	0.0	0.0	0.1	0.7	0.8	3.0
26. Paper products	0.0	0.0	0.0	0.1	0.1	0.4	0.1	0.6	95.2	98.1
27. Printing and publishing	0.0	0.0	0.1	7.1	0.0	0.0	0.1	7.1	1.2	7.9
28. Chemicals	0.2	0.2	0.0	0.9	0.1	0.0	0.3	1.2	3.0	6.1
29. Petroleum and coal products	6.2	6.8	0.3	0.6	0.0	0.1	6.6	7.5	12.9	17.8
30. Rubber and plastic products	0.0	0.1	0.2	3.2	0.0	0.0	0.2	3.3	2.0	6.4
31. Leather products	0.2	1.5	0.7	2.9	0.0	0.0	0.9	4.4	5.7	17.1
32. Stone, clay, and glass products	0.3	0.4	0.2	3.5	0.0	0.0	0.4	3.9	10.4	11.3
33. Primary metal products	1.1	0.8	0.4	3.8	0.2	0.3	1.6	4.8	7.1	15.7
34. Fabricated metal products	0.0	0.1	0.0	2.8	0.0	0.0	0.0	2.9	3.3	6.9
35. Machinery except electrical	0.0	0.1	0.0	1.6	0.0	0.0	0.0	1.7	3.8	8.2
36. Electrical equipment and supplies	0.0	0.5	0.1	7.7	0.0	0.0	0.1	8.2	3.1	11.2
37. Transportation equipment	0.0	0.0	0.0	2.2	0.0	0.0	0.0	2.2	2.1	5.2
38. Instruments	0.0	0.1	0.1	4.3	0.0	0.0	0.1	4.2	9.6	10.4
39. Miscellaneous manufactures	0.1	0.7	1.7	8.2	0.0	0.0	1.8	8.9	7.5	13.5
Total	0.6	0.7	0.5	3.1	0.1	0.1	1.2	3.8	5.5	9.7

Sources: Same as table 3-1.

among the three continents their contributions to change in job potential. Table 3-9 gives the results of this computation.

The total loss of job potential due to increased imports from less developed countries was 295,487 jobs. This is about one-half of the loss in job potential of 593,050 jobs due to imports from all countries between 1963 and 1971 (see table 3-6). Asia is largely responsible for this loss of job potential; in fact, Latin American imports had no effect on U.S. jobs. The most striking losses of job potential occurred in the apparel and electrical equipment and supplies industries. Other sectors that felt a significant impact were primary metal products, transportation equipment, and miscellaneous manufactures. This loss of job potential due to imports from less developed countries amounts to about 42,000 jobs per year. This is equal to approximately 0.2 percent of the labor force in manufacturing and is far less than the potential loss of jobs caused by increased productivity or fluctuations in aggregate demand. Also, these figures refer to imports alone and ignore job expansion brought about by increased exports in both import-competing and export industries.

Summary and Conclusions

The loss in job potential in import-competing industries due to foreign trade has averaged about 44,000 jobs per year—about 0.2 percent of total manufacturing employment and an even more minute fraction of the total U.S. labor force. The loss of job potential due to increased labor productivity was about six to nine times as great as the loss due to foreign trade in import-competing industries. Growth of domestic demand alone has had a favorable impact more than eight times as large as the unfavorable effect of trade.

The estimate of 44,000 jobs lost each year in import-competing industries is quite a bit lower than the AFL-CIO's estimate of jobs lost due to net foreign trade: half a million between 1966 and 1969, or about 170,000 jobs per year. This difference is surprising since the AFL-CIO figures purport to show the net effect of all trade, including exporting industries as well as import-competing industries. Part of the difference, of course, stems from the fact that the 44,000 estimate is based on manufacturing employment only, while the AFL-CIO estimate includes employment in industries where the effect of foreign trade is indirect. Still, it

Table 3-9. *Change in Number of Jobs Available Due to Increased Imports from Less Developed Countries in Selected Import-Competing Industries, 1964–71*

	Less developed countries			
SIC industry class	*Africa*	*Asia*	*Latin America*	*Total*
20. Processed foods	−2,960	−1,913	−36	−4,908
22. Textiles	1	−1,684	−252	−1,934
23. Apparel	−2,647	−51,860	81	−54,426
24. Wood products	−506	−5,482	73	−5,915
25. Furniture	−321	−2,645	1	−2,964
26. Paper products	−6	−71	−169	−245
27. Printing and publishing	0	−1,026	0	−1,026
28. Chemicals	−304	−3,870	−24	−4,197
29. Petroleum and coal products	−2,656	−383	−68	−3,106
30. Rubber and plastic products	−186	−12,194	−4	−12,383
31. Leather products	−3,395	−6,186	−70	−9,650
32. Stone, clay, and glass products	−185	−5,841	−6	−6,032
33. Primary metal products	4,432	−29,474	−437	−25,479
34. Fabricated metal products	−272	−7,940	−4	8,215
35. Machinery except electrical	−872	−11,911	−38	−12,821
36. Electrical equipment and supplies	−5,479	−73,082	70	−78,490
37. Transportation equipment	−612	−33,256	−14	−33,881
38. Instruments	−28	−9,690	0	−9,717
39. Miscellaneous manufactures	−1,606	−18,495	−19	−20,119
Total[a]	−17,582	−276,987	−899	−295,487

Sources: Same as table 3-1.
a. Totals may be slightly off due to rounding.

seems unlikely that those two explanations can fully account for the difference. In any case, even if the AFL-CIO estimates are accepted as valid, 170,000 jobs per year is about 0.2 percent of the total U.S. labor force.

Job losses due to trade are insignificant compared to those due to increased productivity or fluctuations in aggregate demand. This finding is consistent with those of the United Nations Conference on Trade and Development secretariat[13] and the International Labour Office.[14]

13. UN Doc. TD/121/Supp. 1, Jan. 14, 1972, pp. 7–8.

14. "Some Labour Implications of Increased Participation of Developing Countries in Trade in Manufactures and Semi-Manufactures," in UN Doc. TD/97, vol. 3, 1968, pp. 154–55.

The impact of trade with less developed countries on U.S. jobs in import-competing industries is about one-half the total impact of imports in those industries. Tariff preferences for the less developed countries should not have any significant impact on U.S. employment, since much of the increased trade with these countries under any preference scheme would be at the expense of trade with developed countries.

The estimates in this chapter of job loss due to trade do not provide a basis for estimating the number of workers who would be eligible to receive adjustment assistance. For these estimates can include job losses in industries with expanding employment, where employment would have increased more rapidly had there not been increases in imports. Even in an industry with declining employment, the rate of retirements and resignations may be high enough that no particular individual loses his job to trade—there may simply be fewer new workers hired. The number of workers eligible for adjustment assistance programs is estimated in appendix A on the basis of estimated actual losses of jobs by individuals in industries adversely affected by foreign trade.

Finally, in an economy open to foreign trade, there are both opportunities to expand into new markets and costs in contracting production in sectors subject to severe foreign competition. These new opportunities and costs go together: trade policies designed to protect investments and jobs in inefficient industries, by inviting retaliation, may close off export markets and reduce the potential for highly productive jobs in technologically advanced, exporting industries. Thus, the loss of job potential in import-competing industries should be set off against the gain in job opportunities elsewhere in the economy.

CHAPTER FOUR

Early Experience with Adjustment Assistance

BEFORE the passage of the 1962 Trade Expansion Act the only option available to industries and workers injured by import competition was to relate their injury to prior tariff concessions and thereby qualify for escape clause relief. That relief could take the form of increased tariffs or quantitative restrictions. The 1962 act included adjustment assistance as an alternative to escape clause relief to help maintain a competitive economy and full employment without undue protectionism. However, the 1962 legislation tightened the criteria for escape clause action and prescribed equally rigorous standards for eligibility for adjustment assistance. The result was a cumbersome and ineffectual form of adjustment assistance.

The idea of trade adjustment assistance was shortly thereafter applied to trade in automotive products between the United States and Canada. In 1963, in order to stimulate the growth of the automotive industry, Canada introduced a duty remission plan which, under U.S. law, could have been construed as subsidization of exports by the industry to the United States. If this had been determined to be the case, the United States would have been required by law to impose countervailing duties. In turn, Canada most likely would have countered with some form of restrictive action. Negotiations to avoid economic confrontation resulted in an intergovernmental agreement, signed on January 16, 1965, that provided for free trade in automotive products between the United States and Canada, but included explicit safeguards to avoid serious economic dislocation.

The Automotive Products Trade Act of 1965 was designed to implement the agreement.[1]

The agreement prepared the way for substantial shifts in the location of production. Canada was expected to produce large numbers of a more limited range of models and the United States would step up its parts production for shipment to Canada for assembly. The reorganization was expected to lower costs and prices in both countries, but especially in Canada. As the rationalization of production took place, it was expected that a number of automotive plants in the United States would be shut down or that their patterns of production would change. While overall employment in the automotive industry might increase, some workers would be unemployed or would have to be relocated. The agreement received widespread support from U.S. automobile producers, but support from the United Automobile Workers was conditional on more liberal eligibility criteria for adjustment assistance than those of the Trade Expansion Act and on bypassing the Tariff Commission in the determination of eligibility.

Assistance Provisions of the Trade Expansion Act of 1962

Under the 1962 Trade Expansion Act,[2] an industry, a firm, or a group of workers could petition the Tariff Commission for escape clause relief. If the commission found the petitioner eligible for relief, the President could then grant eligibility to apply for adjustment assistance. Workers or firms, but not entire industries, could bypass the escape clause ruling and apply to the Tariff Commission to declare them eligible for adjustment assistance. The criteria used to determine eligibility in both instances required evidence that imports of the article in question were increasing, that the increase was caused "in major part" by a trade concession, and that the increase was the "major cause" of injury to the industry or firms or workers in the industry. Thus, two strong causal connections had to be shown to exist: between trade concessions and the increase of imports, and

1. For a brief history of earlier policy in Canada, see Carl E. Beigie, *The Canada-U.S. Automotive Agreement: An Evaluation* (Washington: National Planning Association; Montreal: Private Planning Association of Canada, 1970), pp. 11–19 and 33–42.

2. 76 Stat., 872-901. The administrative procedures are spelled out in detail in the legislation.

between the increase in imports and the injury that occurred. Because the last major trade legislation had been passed in 1951, and the Kennedy Round of tariff concessions did not begin to take effect until 1968, applicants for relief under the 1962 act were required to prove that injury was due to tariff concessions made some twelve to seventeen years earlier.

In response to a petition for escape clause relief, the Tariff Commission was required to issue its findings within six months. If the commission made an affirmative ruling or took a tie vote, the President could take any combination of the following actions: provide import relief by increasing the tariff on the product in question or by enacting some other import restriction sufficient to prevent or remedy serious injury; authorize groups of workers and firms in the industry in question to apply to the Departments of Labor and Commerce, respectively, for certification of eligibility to receive adjustment assistance. (After an affirmative ruling by the Tariff Commission, if the President did not proclaim import relief within sixty days, he could be required to do so by a majority resolution of both houses of Congress.) Within sixty days of receiving an application for adjustment assistance, Commerce or Labor was to make a ruling on certification of eligibility. Certification required a determination that increased imports had caused serious injury to the petitioning firm or group of workers. In the case of worker petitions, the Department of Labor specified which members of the group of workers applying would be certified and the impact date after which workers had to have been severed in order to be eligible to apply for benefits.

Firms or groups of workers could seek adjustment assistance either directly or while an escape clause relief petition was pending before the Tariff Commission. In either case the commission was obligated to make a ruling within sixty days rather than six months. Upon receiving an affirmative report the firm or group of workers could apply for certification of eligibility to the appropriate executive department. In the case of a tie vote by the commission, the President could authorize the petitioners to apply to the Department of Commerce or Labor for certification of eligibility.

Within two years after certification of eligibility to apply, a firm could file its application for adjustment assistance with the secretary of commerce. Within a reasonable time after filing its application, the firm was required to present a proposal for its economic adjustment. Except for technical assistance in preparing its proposal, a firm could not receive adjustment assistance until the adjustment proposal itself was certified—as opposed to the prior certification of eligibility to apply—by the secretary of commerce. The firm was required to show that the action it proposed could be expected to contribute to its economic adjustment, that it had given adequate consideration to the workers of the firm, and that it would make all reasonable efforts to use its own resources for economic development.

Once the adjustment proposal was certified, the secretary of commerce had to refer the proposal to agencies that he deemed appropriate to furnish the financial and technical assistance sought. Those agencies then examined the proposal and notified the secretary of the assistance they were prepared to furnish. Since the secretary could provide technical and financial assistance only if other agencies stated they were not willing to do so, he had first to determine that assistance was not otherwise available to the firm. In addition to assistance, the secretary could specify tax relief for any firm he determined had sustained a net operating loss in a line of trade that was seriously injured by increased imports.

Workers could apply for regular trade readjustment allowances, for additional readjustment allowances and incidental expenses if they were undergoing retraining, and for relocation allowances. Those who applied for trade readjustment allowances had to be unemployed or substantially underemployed. A worker had to have been gainfully employed for at least 78 of the previous 156 weeks and employed in an adversely affected firm at least 26 of the 52 weeks prior to the beginning of his period of unemployment. He was eligible for allowances only during the two-year period beginning on the impact date specified by the secretary of labor. For workers declared eligible to receive the regular adjustment allowance, additional allowances were granted for those in training programs approved by the secretary of labor. Relocation allowances were given only to heads of families, and only to those who applied while they were eligible to receive readjustment allowances.

The administrative procedures required by statute were numerous and very time-consuming. To summarize, for firms, fourteen steps had to be taken:

1. The firm petitioned the Tariff Commission for either escape clause relief or adjustment assistance.

2. The Tariff Commission held hearings and presented its findings

(within six months for escape clause relief or sixty days for adjustment assistance).

3. The firm applied to the secretary of commerce for certification of eligibility to apply for adjustment assistance.

4. Within sixty days (or thirty days in the case of a direct petition for adjustment assistance) the secretary of commerce issued the certification.

5. The firm filed an application for adjustment assistance with the secretary of commerce.

6. The firm presented an adjustment proposal.

7. The secretary of commerce certified the adjustment proposal.

8. The secretary of commerce submitted the proposal to relevant agencies to seek their technical or financial assistance.

9. The agencies determined the assistance they were willing to furnish.

10. The secretary of commerce determined the precise form and amounts of technical and financial assistance.

11. The firm applied for tax relief.

12. The secretary of commerce certified the application for tax assistance.

13. The certification for tax relief was forwarded to the Internal Revenue Service for implementation.

14. Congress approved any tax rebate of over $100,000.

For workers, the first four steps (but with the secretary of labor issuing certification) were required. Beyond those, the formal procedures were, in principle, simpler, but the procedures for determining eligibility required that large numbers of workers be dealt with individually. Furthermore, adjustment assistance for workers was implemented by state agencies (usually the state agency responsible for unemployment compensation) and required coordination between the Department of Labor and the various state agencies involved.

For both workers and firms, the procedures for obtaining adjustment assistance were time-consuming and expensive. Statutory time limits applied only to Tariff Commission findings. These limits, however, did not significantly reduce the time between trade impact and actual delivery of benefits. Slippages occurred at many points in the process. For example, although the Tariff Commission had to make a ruling within sixty days on adjustment assistance petitions, the date on which the petition was accepted by the commission began the statutory time period. Before a petition could be accepted, however, prescribed forms, which were complicated and lengthy, had to be filed. Small companies and groups of workers often found it difficult to find and assemble the information required. Consequently, the period between the initial informal contact with the Tariff Commission and the final acceptance of a petition was often long. In order to speed up this process, the Tariff Commission in December 1972 simplified the rules governing workers' applications for assistance. The new rules required that they supply only information that would be readily available to them, whereas previously workers had been required to submit information related to the business operations of their firms, which was not generally available to them.

The benefits available to firms consisted of technical assistance, financial assistance in the form of loan guarantees, deferred government participation in loans, direct loans, and tax relief. Technical assistance included assistance in the preparation of adjustment proposals, either by the Department of Commerce, by other government departments or agencies, or by private consulting firms. It was designed principally to pay for consultant services for market research, managerial and financial advice, engineering assistance, help in research and development, and aid in establishing employee training programs.

Financial assistance was given only when other sources were not available to the firm. Loan guarantees and agreements for deferred participations were restricted to 90 percent of the principal. Interest rates on loans and deferred participations could be as low as 4 percent but, in practice, were much higher. Maturities of loans could be as long as twenty-five years.

Tax assistance could be provided by allowing a firm to modify the time distribution of its profits and losses. Ordinarily a firm's operating loss can be applied against operating profits in three previous years to gain a tax credit, or against future profits for five years. Trade-impacted firms were allowed to carry their losses back five years under the Trade Expansion Act.

Benefits to workers included regular readjustment allowances, computed as 65 percent of either the worker's average weekly wage when employed in the trade-impacted firm or the average weekly manufacturing wage, whichever was less. The payments were nontaxable but, combined with any amounts received under unemployment insurance or training allowances received under the Manpower Development and Training Act or other training programs, were not allowed to exceed 75 percent of the worker's previous average weekly wage. The worker was allowed to work while receiving adjustment assistance, but his allowance was reduced by 50 cents for each dollar earned. The maximum period for which regular readjustment allowances were payable was fifty-two weeks (or sixty-five weeks for workers over sixty years old). An additional twenty-six weeks was allowed if the worker was enrolled in a training program approved by the secretary of labor.

There were no separate training programs for trade-impacted workers, but the Department of Labor attempted to place workers in existing manpower training programs. Workers were given supplemental assistance (up to $5 a day) to defray transportation and subsistence expenses when training was provided in facilities beyond commuting distance from their normal place of residence.

A head of family could apply for a relocation allowance if he had a bona fide offer of employment in another location. The relocated worker was provided a subsidy to defray all reasonable expenses incurred in moving his family and household effects, and a lump-sum payment equal to two and one-half times the average weekly manufacturing wage.

Action under the 1962 Act

Between 1962 and late 1969 not one firm or group of workers qualified for adjustment assistance as the result of either an escape clause petition or a direct petition for adjustment assistance. Finally, on November 3, 1969, the Tariff Commission certified a worker petition for adjustment assistance by the employees of a weld mill producing buttweld pipe and tubing. On April 21, 1970, the commission registered a tie vote on a petition for adjustment assistance by a firm that manufactured barber chairs. The firm was then certified to receive adjustment assistance. (There had been a tie vote on October 29, 1965, on a petition by a plywood company, but no certification to apply for assistance was made.) The first affirmative ruling on a petition for escape clause relief was made on December 23, 1969, concerning the piano and piano parts industry.[3] The President authorized the firms and workers in the industry to ask for certification of

3. The petition was separated. An affirmative ruling was given for pianos, and a negative finding was made with respect to piano parts. See U.S. Tariff Commission, "Pianos and Parts Thereof," TC publication 309 (Government Printing Office, 1969), p. 2.

eligibility to apply for adjustment assistance from the Departments of Labor and Commerce. (Prior to November 1969 the Tariff Commission had ruled negatively on thirteen petitions for escape clause relief and six firm petitions and six worker petitions for adjustment assistance.)

From the affirmative ruling in November 1969 until the Trade Expansion Act of 1962 expired on April 3, 1975, the number of affirmative findings and tie votes was substantial: in 8 of 14 escape clause rulings, 25 of 60 rulings on firm petitions for adjustment assistance, and 95 of 260 rulings on worker petitions for adjustment assistance.[4] The commission made 40 affirmative findings out of the 76 worker petitions presented between November 3, 1969, and April 16, 1971; after that date the number of worker petitions increased, while the proportion of affirmative rulings or tie votes declined: only 55 of 178 rulings were affirmative or tie votes.

The lack of affirmative votes by the Tariff Commission before 1969 reflected in part the scarcity of petitions for escape clause relief or adjustment assistance. During most of the early and middle sixties the economy was booming. As the trade balance became less favorable and the economy became relatively stagnant in the late sixties and early seventies, instances of injury to firms and workers arose more frequently. The fact that the commission's findings were negative until late 1969 may also have discouraged applications.

Before 1968, very few tariff concessions were being made because the Kennedy Round tariff cuts had not yet begun. The Trade Expansion Act's provision that increased imports be caused "in major part" by tariff concessions made affirmative findings difficult. Before passage of the 1962 act, escape clause relief could be granted if increased imports were due "in whole or in part" to tariff concessions.[5] The Tariff Commission usually had presumed this condition to be met if there were a mere coincidence of a prior concession and an injury. The 1962 wording, however, was often interpreted to require a closer coincidence in time of tariff concessions and increased imports. Murray and Egmand believe that this test had an instrumental effect on the commission's decisions.[6]

4. The tally reflects the actual number of rulings, counting each separate ruling where single petitions were divided. Tariff Commission reports classify divided petitions under one numerical heading.

5. Reciprocal Trade Agreements Extension Act of 1951, cited in Tracy W. Murray and Michael R. Egmand, "Full Employment, Trade Expansion, and Adjustment Assistance," *Southern Economic Journal*, vol. 36 (April 1970), p. 405.

6. Ibid., p. 415.

Affirmative findings were also made difficult by the requirement that increased imports be a "major factor" in causing injury. Before 1962, increased imports had to "contribute substantially" to injury. The phrase "major factor" was most often interpreted to mean the factor that not only exerted the greatest influence on the result, but that influenced the result more than all other factors combined. This is a very stringent criterion, since usually a host of factors is operating to cause injury, so that more often than not there may be no major factor.

The greater incidence of tie and affirmative votes after 1969 can be attributed in part to the Kennedy Round tariff cuts, which began to take effect in 1968. The number of petitions for escape clause relief or adjustment assistance increased markedly—from one in 1968 to ninety-one in 1971, with the greatest increase in the number of worker petitions. The most important factor, however, was the shift in reasoning by the members of the Tariff Commission in interpreting the statutory criteria. That turned on their intepretation of the time interval between the granting of tariff concessions and increases in imports. In three worker petitions decided affirmatively in late 1969, involving a buttweld pipe mill and two factories assembling transmission towers, the majority members of the commission argued that the cumulative effect of all prior tariff concessions should be considered, and that the question should be asked whether "except for the concessions" imports could "have reached substantially the level" currently attained.[7] In these investigations, not only was the time lag less significant, but the interpretation of "in major part" was shifted from meaning "more important than all other factors combined" to meaning "except for"—a considerably more lenient test of cause.

Similarly, in determining whether increased imports were the "major factor" in causing injury, the reasoning changed from time to time. Some commissioners ruled affirmatively on this test if they could conclude that there had been "no other specific, significant, timely changes in the situation," and then could presume that increased imports had been the major factor in causing the injury.[8] A stricter interpretation would require all

7. U.S. Tariff Commission, *Buttweld Pipe: Workers of the Weld Mill, Ambridge, Pa. Plant, Armco Steel Corporation,* TC publication 297 (GPO, 1969), pp. 10–11. The commission's shift in viewpoint is discussed in Murray and Egmand, "Full Employment, Trade Expansion, and Adjustment Assistance," p. 410.

8. See the minority view in U.S. Tariff Commission, *Ceramic Floor and Wall Tile,* TC publication 145 (GPO, 1964), pp. 23–24.

other factors, whether significant or not, to be weighed together and compared to increased imports as a causal influence.

There were also various degrees of interpretation concerning "serious injury" and the meaning of articles "like or directly competitive with" the product in question. For example, in petitions involving piano parts and heels and soles for shoes, it was ruled that like or directly competitive articles were not being imported in increased quantities sufficient to cause injury. What, in fact, occurred was an increase in imports of the end products—pianos and shoes—so that the domestic demand for parts of pianos and shoes was reduced. However, some commissioners found it difficult to construe the law as covering injury caused indirectly by increased imports.[9]

The commissioners became receptive to the more lenient interpretations—some more so than others—and the findings after late 1969 were determined to a large extent by the makeup of the Tariff Commission and which members were present and voting on particular cases.[10] For example, Commissioner Bruce E. Clubb, who served on the commission from July 1967 until June 16, 1971, and Commissioner George M. Moore, who assumed office in August 1969, were remarkably consistent in being on the affirmative side in tie votes or affirmative rulings. They were joined periodically by other members of the commission, most often by Commissioner Penelope Thunberg until she left the commission in June 1970. Between June 1970 and April 1971, there were quite a number of petitions, but in most cases only four commissioners voted. Commissioners Clubb and Moore voted most often in the affirmative and were occasionally joined by Chairman Glenn Sutton. After Commissioner Clubb became inactive in May of 1971, Commissioner Moore's was frequently the only affirmative vote, and for a time very few affirmative rulings emerged. As new members were added to the commission, they refrained from voting at first. By the spring of 1972, however, a stable

9. See U.S. Tariff Commission, *Heels, Soles and Soling Sheets: Goodyear Tire and Rubber Co., Windsor, Vt.,* TC publication 441 (GPO, 1971), *Heels for Womens Shoes: Service Heel Co., Lawrence, Mass.,* TC publication 461 (GPO, 1972), *Sole Leather, Lining, and Welting Leathers: Former Workers of the Elkland Leather Company, Inc., Elkland, Pennsylvania,* TC publication 520, and *Pianos and Parts Thereof,* TC publication 309.

10. The calendar of Tariff Commission decisions under the Trade Expansion Act, including the votes of the various commissioners, is on file in the Office of the Secretary of the International Trade Commission.

voting pattern again emerged. Commissioners Moore, Catherine Bedell, and Joseph Parker voted most often in the affirmative and Commissioners William Leonard and J. Banks Young most often in the negative, making a majority in favor of a less strict interpretation of the statutory criteria. Commissioner Italo Ablondi, who became a member in June 1972, supported a number of workers' petitions but never voted in the affirmative on any firm petition. The liberal side was strengthened in late 1974, when Commissioner Daniel Minchew replaced Commissioner Young and voted consistently in the affirmative in nonunanimous decisions.

Adjustment Assistance to Firms

By April 3, 1975, when the Trade Expansion Act expired, thirty-eight firms had requested certification of eligibility for adjustment assistance, having qualified to do so through Tariff Commission findings of injury in cases of either industry petitions for escape clause relief or firm petitions for adjustment assistance.[11] As tables 4-1 and 4-2 show, thirty-six firms were certified; two were denied certifications. Of those firms certified, six were not expected to submit adjustment proposals. Only nineteen had submitted proposals, had them approved by the Commerce Department, and actually been authorized to receive assistance when the Trade Expansion Act expired.

More requests for certification came from firms in the shoe industry than from any other industry. The piano industry ranked second and the textile industry third in number of requests. Applications from both the textile and shoe industries resulted from individual firm petitions to the Tariff Commission for adjustment assistance, while the numerous requests from the piano industry were a result of the escape clause ruling for the piano industry, allowing all firms in the industry to apply. Most of the applicants were very small firms, although there were some exceptions, including two firms in the glass industry that had sales of $50 million to $60 million. All but one of the eligible firms came from the older industrial areas in the eastern and midwestern parts of the United States, and from the South, where the textile companies' petitions arose. Massachusetts had the most firms certified—five shoe companies and one electronics firm.

11. See U.S. Department of Commerce, Office of Trade Adjustment Assistance, "Case Summary" (July 10, 1975; processed).

Table 4-1. *Department of Commerce Action on Adjustment Assistance to Firms, December 1969 to April 2, 1975*

Item	*Petition approved by Tariff Commission*	*Eligibility certified by Commerce*	*Proposal submitted and certified*
Industry			
Shoes	11	11	6
Pianos	6	5	2
Textiles	5	5	3
Granite and marble	4	4	0
Consumer electronics	2	2	1
Electronic components	2	2	2
Stainless steel flatware	2	2	1
Glass	2	2	2
Ball bearings	1	1	0
Data processing	1	1	1
Barber chairs	1	1	1
Earthenware	1	0	0
Total	38	36	19
Year			
1969	8	0	0
1970	4	7	2
1971	11	9	4
1972	7	6	5
1973	4	9	4
1974	3	3	4
1975	1	2	0

Source: U.S. Department of Commerce, Office of Trade Adjustment Assistance, "Case Summary" (July 10, 1975; processed).

The elapsed time between the finding of injury and the authorization of benefits averaged about seventeen months, with the longest case taking almost thirty-eight months. The points at which the delays occurred varied.[12] In some instances there was a long period between the time of the Tariff Commission finding and the certification of eligibility. In others the time between the submission of an adjustment proposal and the acceptance of the proposal was almost a year. In still others the firm itself was tardy in submitting adjustment proposals after receiving certification of eligibility. The time lag was very much influenced by whether a particular firm or a whole industry had petitioned the Tariff Commission for

12. *Wall Street Journal*, Dec. 8, 1971.

Table 4-2. *Department of Commerce Authorizations for Trade Adjustment Assistance, through April 2, 1975*
Thousands of dollars

Item	Pre-proposal technical assistance	Technical assistance	Financial assistance[a]	Tax reductions	Total
Industry					
Glass	...	...	14,000.0	...	14,000.0
Shoes	220.2[b]	660.0	12,228.5	79.4	13,188.3
Textiles	180.7	100.0	3,960.0	3,358.4	7,599.1
Barber chairs	...	35.2	3,784.4	...	3,819.6
Pianos	19.4	136.0	3,269.0	...	3,424.5
Electronic components	20.5	100.0	1,713.0	...	1,833.5
Stainless steel flatware	5.0	150.0	600.0	...	755.0
Consumer electronics	2.5	...	...	233.8	236.3
Data processing	...	...	...	153.2	153.2
Granite and marble	142.8	...	...	...	142.8
Ball bearings	33.9	...	...	...	33.9
Total	625.0	1,181.4	39,554.8	3,824.8	45,186.2
Year					
1970	16.9	285.2	5,224.4	9.4	5,535.9
1971	17.5	166.0	4,672.0	233.8	5,089.4
1972	51.3	196.0	5,708.0	3,581.6	9,436.9
1973	332.4	150.0	9,053.2	...	9,535.7
1974	116.4	414.2	11,837.3	...	12,367.9
1975	33.9	...	3,060.0	...	3,093.9

Source: Same as table 4-1. Totals may be uneven because of rounding.
a. Particularly in this category, disbursements did not always equal the authorization. For example, American Girl Fashions (shoes) received only $1.35 million of its authorized financial assistance of $5.1 million, and the E. J. Paidar Co. received only $2.7 million out of $3.8 million authorized; both firms failed before their proposals could be fully implemented.
b. Includes a $56,482 industry study commissioned by the Commerce Department and not charged to any individual firms.

relief. In the case of industry petitions for escape clause relief, the certification procedure was more lengthy since the Department of Commerce had to determine whether a particular firm applying for certification had been injured. When a firm had already received an affirmative Tariff Commission finding, the Department of Commerce certification was largely pro forma. The delays were often caused by difficulties and disagreements within the Department of Commerce concerning such decisions as whether creditors should be paid off with federal loans, what contributions could be expected from wealthy shareholders, and whether there was a reasonable assurance of repayment—issues on which the trade legislation provided only limited guidance.

The shortest case on record was that of the Emil J. Paidar Company, a manufacturer of barber chairs. The time between the Tariff Commission's injury finding and the authorization of assistance was just under four months. In this case, however, the company had had a long history of seeking assistance. On July 21, 1967, the barber chair industry applied for escape clause relief, but the Tariff Commission was unanimous in its negative decision.[13] The Paidar Company then applied separately for adjustment assistance on November 13, 1967. In a three–two decision, this petition was also denied.[14] In December 1969 the industry and the company again applied for escape clause relief and adjustment assistance. In both cases the Tariff Commission was deadlocked, but the President approved adjustment assistance although not escape clause relief. The Paidar Company adjustment proposal to shift production to dental cabinets was submitted only nine days after the certification of eligibility. Three weeks later the company was authorized to receive almost $4 million in financial and technical assistance. The firm was not able to survive, however, and in early 1972 filed a petition for bankruptcy.

A total of about $41 million in financial and technical adjustment assistance was authorized for firms. No assistance was given until 1970, when about $5.5 million was authorized. In the peak year, 1974, about $12.5 million in technical and financial assistance was authorized. Tax assistance grew rapidly from negligible amounts in 1970 and 1971 to $3.6 million in 1972, but fell to zero thereafter. Most of the financial assistance was in the form of loans, whose interest rates were set at the U.S. Treasury annual average borrowing rate for each range of maturities. Three loan guarantees were authorized. Arrangements with private lending institutions were hard to make, however. Most banks are not willing to lend at maturities in the range of fifteen to twenty-five years—the maturities of loans under adjustment assistance certifications. Guaranteed interest rates were required by statute to be no more than 1 percent, or

13. See U.S. Tariff Commission, *Barbers' Chairs,* TC publication 228 (GPO, 1968), p. 3.

14. See U.S. Tariff Commission, *Barbers' Chairs: Emil J. Paidar Co.,* TC publication 229 (GPO, 1968), p. 4. In dissenting, Commissioners Thunberg and Clubb argued that while the industry (which contained two firms) as a whole was not injured, Paidar Company was in fact injured (pp. 24 and 48–49).

2 percent in exceptional cases, greater than the government cost of borrowing. Such interest rates were often lower than those that could be obtained from less risky prime customers. Also, guarantees could cover no more than 90 percent of the principal; thus, private lenders were usually unwilling to lend to highly risky borrowers at a relatively low rate.

Adjustment Assistance to Workers

Between December 1969 and April 2, 1975, 110 groups of workers were certified by the Department of Labor to receive adjustment assistance.[15] About 54,000 workers were involved, of whom about 35,000 actually received benefits; most received readjustment allowances only. About $86 million was spent on readjustment allowances; only about $3 million was allocated to training under the provisions of the 1962 act. About 10 percent of all workers assisted received placement services or training, and fewer than 125 workers received relocation allowances (59 of these were given to one particular group of workers).[16]

Of the 110 petitions certified, 95 stemmed from direct applications to the Tariff Commission and 15 were the result of workers' group petitions subsequent to Tariff Commission findings of injury in four industry petitions for escape clause relief. By far the greatest number of certifications involved the shoe industry (see table 4-3). This is reflected in the geographical distribution of certifications: 22 originated in Massachusetts, six of them in one town (Haverhill). No other state had more than 13 certifications. Cases were widely dispersed by states but were, with very few exceptions, east of the Mississippi River.

The elapsed time between the impact date and the issuance of certification averaged about twenty-two months.[17] The shortest interval was about two and one-half months and the longest was fifty-seven months. Since the longest possible period of eligibility for readjustment allowances was eighteen months, the average period between the impact date and

15. Data on the disposition of worker adjustment assistance petitions are on file at U.S. Department of Labor, Bureau of International Labor Affairs.

16. Unpublished data provided by the Bureau of International Labor Affairs (July 1975).

17. This is an increase in the average of 16 months reported for the first 29 certifications. See Marvin Fooks, "Trade Adjustment Assistance," *United States International Economic Policy in an Interdependent World*, papers submitted to U.S. Commission on International Trade and Investment Policy (GPO, 1971), p. 350.

Table 4-3. *Adjustment Assistance Certifications by Department of Labor, October 1972 to April 2, 1975*

Industry	*Direct petitions affirmed by Tariff Commission*	*Petitions resulting from escape clause rulings*	*Total*
Footwear	51	...	51
Electronics	24	...	24
Musical instruments and parts	4	7	11
Textiles	6	...	6
Glass	...	5	5
Granite and marble	2	2	4
Stainless steel holloware and flatware	3	...	3
Fabricated steel products	2	...	2
Automotive products	2	...	2
Industrial equipment	1	...	1
Ceramic tableware	...	1	1
Total	95	15	110

Source: U.S. Department of Labor, Bureau of International Labor Affairs.

certification exceeded the maximum benefit period. Not all workers, however, were severed at the impact date, and some workers received benefits long after the group of workers to which they belonged was certified. Individual worker certification and delivery of benefits were administered by state agencies, so it frequently took some time before workers actually received their readjustment allowances. A Department of Labor survey of a sample of workers taken in 1970 indicated that the average elapsed time between group certification and individual worker certification was about fifteen weeks. An average of seven additional weeks passed before workers received their first checks. On the other hand, most workers were severed some time after the impact date, so that the time between separation and group certification averaged only thirty-three weeks. Thus, about fifty-five weeks elapsed between the time a worker was separated and the time he received his first check.

Most workers found some employment in the year after they were severed, so that few received the full fifty-two weeks of payment. Most workers, however, found relatively unstable interim employment, and they were allowed to resume their eligibility for trade readjustment allowances after once again becoming unemployed. Normally, eligibility could resume at any time up to two years after the date of group certification, although it could resume up to six years later for workers who were re-employed in the trade-impacted firm.

Workers sampled by the Department of Labor generally received an initial lump-sum payment, averaging about $745, which in about 10 percent of the cases exhausted the benefits to which the worker was entitled. The average worker received a trade readjustment allowance for thirty weeks and had been eligible for only seventeen weeks of unemployment insurance. The average worker in the sample was about forty-four years old, had an eighth grade education, and at the time of the survey received a wage of only about $2.65 an hour. More than half the workers were women and more than 90 percent were white. Thus, the workers who received adjustment assistance can be characterized as generally older, unskilled, poorly educated, and poorly paid.[18]

The Canadian-American Automotive Agreement

The Automotive Products Trade Act of 1965 had much more liberal eligibility criteria for adjustment assistance than the Trade Expansion Act of 1962. In order for a group of workers or a firm to be eligible under the automotive act there must have been actual or threatened "dislocation" of the petitioning firm or workers; and the operation of the agreement must have been a "primary factor" in causing this dislocation.

Under the law, a decrease in domestic production, together with either an appreciable decrease in exports to Canada greater than any increase in Canadian production of the good, or an increase in imports from Canada, was regarded as prima facie evidence that the operation of the agreement was a primary cause of the dislocation.[19] However, this was not necessarily the only way in which the operation of the agreement could cause dislocation. For example, production might shift from one plant to another within the United States as part of the production rationalization expected under the act, or a parts manufacturer might lose sales as a result of the shutdown of a particular plant it was supplying.

The power to determine eligibility was vested by the President in the Automotive Agreement Adjustment Board, whose membership consisted

18. There was little difference in the characteristics of workers in and outside the shoe industry, except that more than 60 percent of the shoe workers were women and the average length of service in trade-impacted shoe firms was 6.7 years, compared to 10.4 years' service for other workers.

19. 79 Stat. 1019.

of the secretaries of commerce, labor, and the treasury. Petitions for adjustment assistance were made directly to the board, which forwarded them to the Tariff Commission. The role of the Tariff Commission was purely a fact-finding one with regard to the two eligibility criteria, and the board was not bound by the Tariff Commission's findings.

The eligibility criteria for adjustment assistance under the automotive act were more liberal than the trade act eligibility requirements in several respects. While it was required that the operation of the automotive products agreement be adjudged a "primary factor" in causing dislocation, this was interpreted to mean "a factor which is greater in importance than any other single factor present in a given case, but which does not have to be greater than any combination of other factors."[20] There was no need to show a causal relationship between an increase in imports and dislocation. If dislocation occurred at the same time as an appreciable increase in imports, it could be presumed that the dislocation was caused by the increase in imports. Moreover, the criteria included a decrease in exports as well as an increase in imports. This was to take account of the fact that U.S. export production might be shifted to Canada. And even when there was no change in domestic production or trade, eligibility could be affirmed if the operation of the agreement caused the dislocation.

Also, the vague language of the statute allowed for considerable administrative flexibility in determining eligibility. In the case of workers, the law required only "unemployment or underemployment of a significant number or proportion of the workers of such firm."[21] The Automotive Agreement Adjustment Board defined "significant unemployment" as 5 percent of the workers or fifty workers in one firm, whichever was less.[22] The statutory language regarding an appreciable increase in imports or decrease in exports was also vague. "Appreciable" could be defined by the board, although in fact the legislative history of the act provided guidance that was followed by the board and the Tariff Commission. The House committee report directed that the 1964 model year be used as a base period and noted that a change in production, imports, or exports of more than 5 percent over the most recent three or four months would be considered appreciable.

Adjustment assistance benefits were the same under the automotive

20. Cited in Jeffrey A. Manley, "Adjustment Assistance: Experience Under the Automotive Products Trade Act of 1965," *Harvard International Law Journal,* vol. 10 (Spring 1969), p. 301.

21. 76 Stat. 884.

22. Manley, "Adjustment Assistance," p. 301.

products and trade acts: financial, technical, and tax assistance for firms, and readjustment allowances, training and training allowances, and relocation benefits for workers. The adjustment assistance authority of the automotive act was limited to a three-year period. Petitions had to be filed between January 20, 1966, and June 30, 1968. Within sixty days after receipt and publication of a petition, the board was required to make a ruling. In all, twenty-one groups of workers filed petitions—none were filed by firms—and fourteen were certified by the board as eligible.[23]

The fourteen successful petitions represented 2,493 workers; the 1,943 found eligible for assistance payments[24] represented 0.3 percent of the 1964 work force in the industry. Over half of the workers who were certified as eligible became unemployed when relatively small plants of major independent automobile and parts producers were shifted to Canada. Other certifications involved assembly operations directly related to the rationalization process. The average worker received twenty weeks of readjustment allowances and small retraining benefits. The total expenditures amounted to $4.1 million,[25] or about $2,100 per eligible worker. Nearly all of the expenditures went for readjustment allowances rather than for retraining or relocation benefits.

Conclusions

The trade adjustment assistance program of the 1962 Trade Expansion Act was an abysmal failure, while the worker adjustment program under the Canadian-American Automotive Agreement was a modest success. The major advantages of the automotive program came from the more easily satisfied set of eligibility criteria and the determination of eligibility by the Automotive Agreement Adjustment Board rather than the Tariff Commission, which resulted in speedier decisions. Because the criteria were flexible and because all petitions dealt with only a few firms in the automotive industry, the board had to gather relatively few data on a

23. Out of the twelve petitions that met the economic criteria, only three did not meet the "primary cause" of dislocations test. Of the nine groups that did not meet the economic criteria, the board certified five as eligible, ruling that the "operation of the APTA" had been the "primary cause" of their dislocation. See ibid., p. 303.

24. James Jonish, "Adjustment Assistance Experience under the U.S.-Canadian Automotive Agreement," *Industrial and Labor Relations Review*, vol. 23 (July 1970), p. 557.

25. Fooks, "Trade Adjustment Assistance," p. 352.

small potential set of firms. The program's focus on a few firms in a one-union industry also made it likely that petitions would be filed quickly, since potential petitioners would be likely to be aware of the program and be able to draw on accumulated experience in filing petitions. Furthermore, the board, composed of cabinet members, may possibly have shown more practical concern for speedy determination than the Tariff Commission members, chosen for their legal expertise and given to careful arguments over fine points of law.

Lapses of time between injury and delivery of benefits occurred in part because the Department of Labor had to pass authority for the actual delivery of benefits to state unemployment compensation and employment service facilities. This problem was particularly acute under the Trade Expansion Act program because it operated in so many states.

Neither act's provisions for manpower training and employment services were utilized to any great degree. A major obstacle to their use was a lack of separate authorizations and appropriations for them. The goals and priorities of manpower training and employment services are set by law and administrative direction, and it is not easy to divert programs to focus specifically on trade-impacted workers unless separate appropriations, under the control of the adjustment assistance program administrators, are available.

The 1962 act's adjustment assistance program for firms was particularly unsuccessful. It was hampered by so many deficiencies in the law that even the best efforts of the Department of Commerce administrators failed to build an effective program. For one thing, the criteria for eligibility were so strict that only the sickest, most poorly managed, and most unfortunate firms were declared eligible. Such firms are particularly difficult to help—even 90 percent loan guarantees were not enough to encourage private money-lenders to provide loans on the kind of terms necessary to resuscitate these firms. The program should have been modified toward broader eligibility so that help could have gone to firms for which rehabilitation was more feasible.

Another factor inhibiting the Trade Expansion Act program for firms was the unreasonably large number of administrative steps and procedures required by law. The program is a classic case of legal requirements designed to prevent abuse greatly reducing the effectiveness of the measures authorized by law.

CHAPTER FIVE

Assistance under the Trade Act of 1974

BEFORE the passage of the Trade Act of 1974 there was a clear need for a more effective trade adjustment assistance program, since the Trade Expansion Act had accomplished little in that area. If anything, the provisions of the 1962 act discouraged rather than encouraged resource mobility. Few retraining or relocation benefits were dispensed, while the greatest benefits to workers came largely from extra unemployment compensation. The program neither substantially improved worker security nor provided effective compensation to those injured by trade. Benefits often went to firms on the verge of failure or already operationally moribund, while more progressive and ably managed firms in trade-impacted industries were not assisted, since they were less likely to show the adverse effects of import competition.

The injury criteria were so strict that the Tariff Commission made few affirmative rulings, although the record improved after 1969. The process of determining benefits encouraged long delays and bureaucratic indecision. Organized labor saw the program as ill designed to meet present realities, and the business community was suspicious of the formidable bureaucratic difficulties that firms encountered in applying for adjustment assistance.[1]

1. *Wall Street Journal,* Dec. 8, 1971.

The obvious inadequacies spawned many proposals for change[2] and a raft of bills was introduced into Congress. None of these passed until President Nixon introduced a trade reform bill early in 1973, which was finally passed in substantially modified form late in the following year as the Trade Act of 1974. This act brought a number of sweeping changes to the trade adjustment assistance program.

Eligibility Criteria

Under the Trade Expansion Act of 1962, the eligibility criteria for trade adjustment assistance and for escape clause relief were identical, and very strict in requiring both that increased imports be a major factor in causing injury to a firm or industry and that a prior tariff concession be the major cause of that increase in imports. The Trade Act of 1974 specifies different criteria for escape clause relief and for adjustment assistance and has substantially liberalized both sets of criteria.

The criteria for escape clause relief include no reference to prior tariff concessions and specify only that increased imports be a "substantial cause" of serious injury to the domestic industry. A substantial cause need only be more important than any other single cause, while the "major cause" it replaced required that the cause have a greater impact than all other causes combined.

A firm or group of workers is eligible for adjustment assistance on the basis of a set of prima facie criteria—it is not necessary to prove serious injury directly. It need only be shown that a significant number of workers have lost their jobs, the firm's sales have decreased, imports have in-

2. See Special Representative for Trade Negotiations, *Future United States Foreign Trade Policy* (Government Printing Office, 1969), pp. 41–59; U.S. Commission on International Trade and Investment Policy, *United States International Economic Policy in an Interdependent World* (GPO, 1971), pp. 45–69; National Association of Manufacturers, International Economic Affairs Department, "Trade Adjustment Assistance: United States International Competitiveness and Implications for Domestic Adjustment Policy" (NAM, February 1973; processed); National Planning Association Advisory Committee, *U.S. Foreign Economic Policy for the 1970s: A New Approach to New Realities,* planning pamphlet 130 (Washington: NPA, 1971), pp. 18–57; statement by Chamber of Commerce of the United States, in *Trade Reform,* hearings before the House Committee on Ways and Means, 93:1 (GPO, 1973), pt. 5, pp. 1373–1409; and *Trade Adjustment Assistance,* hearings before the Subcommittee on Foreign Economic Policy of the House Committee on Foreign Affairs, 92:2 (GPO, 1972).

creased, and increased imports "contributed importantly" to the loss of jobs.

Under the 1962 Trade Expansion Act, not only were the criteria identical for adjustment assistance and escape clause relief, but initial findings of eligibility for both were made by the Tariff Commission. Under the 1974 act, the criteria for adjustment assistance are more liberal than those for escape clause relief and the responsibility for determining eligibility for assistance is assigned to different agencies.

The more liberal nature of the criteria for adjustment assistance is implicit in the requirement that imports contribute "importantly" to the loss of jobs, contrasted with the requirement that an industry seeking escape clause relief show that increased imports are a "substantial cause" of injury. According to the law, "importantly" is an easier standard than "substantially," for "a cause may have contributed importantly even though it contributed less than another single cause."[3] *The intent of Congress is clearly to encourage the use of adjustment assistance in preference to import restrictions as a means of relief from injury due to imports.*

Escape clause relief is the responsibility of the International Trade Commission (the former Tariff Commission), while the secretary of labor or of commerce determines eligibility for adjustment assistance. The International Trade Commission has up to six months to make its determinations; the secretaries must act within sixty days. Requests for adjustment assistance therefore appear more attractive than requests for escape clause relief, both because of the shorter, legally stipulated processing time and because the quasi-legal proceedings of the International Trade Commission might be as cumbersome and time-consuming as were those of the Tariff Commission. The Departments of Labor and Commerce are more likely to expedite delivery to workers and firms, respectively, who tend to be the clients of those departments. Furthermore, when the International Trade Commission makes a positive finding, it may recommend adjustment assistance rather than import restrictions as a remedy. And even when the commission suggests that only import restrictions can relieve injury from imports, the President may recommend adjustment assistance.

One obstacle to the use of adjustment assistance under the 1962 act was its applicability to individual firms. Escape clause relief, antidumping

3. *Trade Reform Act of 1973,* report of the House Committee on Ways and Means (GPO, 1973), pp. 53–54.

provisions, and countervailing duties applied to industries, which tended to make them, politically speaking, a more likely choice of relief than adjustment assistance. A whole industry can press for restrictive forms of import relief while only a few firms in the industry are likely to be eligible for adjustment assistance. Furthermore, an entire industry would probably have greater political impact than any single firm. Possibly, adjustment assistance would be more willingly used if, at least in part, eligibility findings were based on the industry's position. Some European programs with that focus have been reasonably successful. The Canadian-American Automotive Agreement's adjustment assistance program had such an orientation, which in part accounts for its success. The 1974 Trade Act, however, leaves findings on adjustment assistance on an individual firm basis and escape clause relief on an industry basis.

Imports can increase in either absolute or relative terms for an industry to meet one of the criteria for escape clause relief or adjustment assistance. The law, however, overlooks the situation in industries that import but also have some export trade. In such a situation the criterion should apply to net imports—the excess of imports over exports. For example, if imports in an industry increase but exports are increasing even faster, then that industry should have little claim to either escape clause relief or adjustment assistance, since the net effect of trade on its sales is positive.

Another continuing inequity in the eligibility criteria for adjustment assistance is the exclusion from eligibility of firms that are major suppliers of import-competing firms.[4] For example, manufacturers of soles and heels for shoes have been denied assistance even though the shoe firms they supplied were eligible. A simple rule of thumb could be applied to allow eligibility for firms indirectly affected by imports. Any firm, for example, that sells 50 percent or more of its output to trade-impacted firms could be made eligible for adjustment assistance.[5]

A number of bills introduced in Congress before the passage of the 1974 trade act would have considered workers eligible for adjustment assistance when their employer closed a plant in the United States and at approximately the same time opened a foreign plant producing similar

4. The adjustment assistance program of the Canadian-American Automotive Agreement does allow automotive part suppliers to receive assistance.

5. Theoretically, the total indirect effect of import competition on a firm could be measured through input-output analysis. It is not feasible to do so, however, because of difficulties in providing accurate input-output tables, in matching industrial categories to input-output coefficients, and in performing the calculations on a continuing basis.

or like products. Although the 1974 act does not offer assistance to the victims of runaway plants, the President, in a message accompanying the administration's trade bill in 1973, did recognize the problem and pledged to seek reform in the tax law that would reduce incentives for firms to relocate plants abroad. Congress did include provisions in the trade act governing the behavior of multinational corporations, however. Every firm must notify workers likely to be affected by a move abroad, as well as the secretaries of labor and commerce, at least sixty days before the date of the move. Furthermore, the act expresses the sense of Congress that every firm should encourage its workers to apply for adjustment assistance or other employment opportunities, and assist in relocating workers who lose their jobs.

Benefits for Workers and Firms

The level of benefits for workers is substantially higher under the Trade Act of 1974 than under the 1962 act. The trade readjustment allowance as a percentage of a workers' weekly wage has been raised from 65 percent to 70 percent, and, more important, the maximum payment has risen from 65 percent to 100 percent of the average weekly wage in manufacturing. Furthermore, workers are eligible if they have worked 26 out of the last 52 weeks in a trade-impacted firm, but no longer have to have been employed during 78 of the previous 156 weeks.

Also, eligible workers are given somewhat more freedom to engage in part-time work. Formerly the trade readjustment allowance, combined with extra earned income, was not allowed to exceed 70 percent of the worker's former average weekly wage. Now a worker may keep 50 percent of other income earned, until total income exceeds 80 percent of his average weekly wage or 130 percent of the average weekly wage in manufacturing, whichever is less. This arrangement provides an incentive for the worker to seek part-time employment, but a great disincentive to seek full-time employment, because of the way in which the marginal tax rates work.[6]

6. The laid-off worker who had been earning $100 per week would receive weekly adjustment assistance benefits of $70. His additional earnings up to $20 would have a marginal tax rate of 50 percent. More than $20 of extra earned income, however, combined with his adjustment assistance benefits, would cause him to exceed 80 percent of his former weekly wage—the marginal tax rate on his earnings over $20 would be greater than 100 percent because they would be subject to both income

The adjustment assistance benefits for firms have remained roughly the same, though the tax assistance that was available under the Trade Expansion Act has been abolished. Technical assistance, loans, and loan guarantees may still be provided under the 1974 act. Also, procedures for certifying proposals for adjustment assistance have been simplified and the conditions attached to granting assistance to firms have been relaxed. For example, the law no longer requires the secretary of commerce to determine what help other agencies can give, and working capital needs may now be considered to be equally as important as investment in plant and equipment in approved assistance plans.

The Older Worker

Workers over sixty years old have been recognized as a special problem and been made eligible for twenty-six more weeks of assistance than younger workers. The victims of import competition are generally older workers. For example, in a survey conducted by the Department of Labor, the average age of workers awarded trade readjustment allowances was forty-four. Although the survey included many former shoe workers in New England, their age distribution did not differ greatly from that of other workers surveyed in the glass, table utensils, textiles, electronics, and musical instruments industries. The former workers of the Libbey-Owens-Ford glass plant in Shreveport, Louisiana, were particularly old—the average length of service was twenty-five and a half years. If these workers had been dropped from the sample survey, the average age of those surveyed would have decreased slightly, to about forty-three.

Ordinarily, the ranks of unemployed in the United States are filled by younger workers or individuals with limited or no recent experience in the labor force. That is true because layoffs occur first among workers with limited seniority rights.[7] Trade-impacted workers, however, are generally older because their layoffs usually are due to plant closings in old or de-

---

taxes and the dollar-for-dollar reduction in the adjustment allowance. When his extra earnings exceeded $80, he would no longer be entitled to adjustment benefits.

7. Some recent collective bargaining arrangements, however, require employers to offer those with the highest seniority the option of being laid off, in preference to workers with less seniority. If layoff periods are expected to be short and unemployment benefits are sufficiently high, some senior employees may elect to be laid off. If this trend becomes important, it could change the profile of the average unemployed worker.

clining industries. For some time before firms with declining sales are shut down, they hire relatively few new workers. Thus when the firm does close, the average age and experience of workers is high. When the Studebaker Corporation closed its South Bend operation in 1963, the average age of the workers was fifty-four.[8] In the 1956 closing of the Packard automobile operation in Detroit, 95 percent of the workers were over forty years old and two-thirds had twenty-three years or more of seniority.[9] In the meat packing plants shut down by Armour and Company in the early sixties, the median age ranged from forty-five to forty-eight.[10] It is unusual, in fact, to find cases in which the average age of workers fired in a plant closing is less than forty.

Those older workers whose employment is terminated by plant closings have considerably more difficulty than young workers in finding jobs. Furthermore, when older workers do find jobs, they are often paid less.[11]

The provisions for older workers in theTrade Act of 1974 are relatively modest. Their needs could better be taken into account if the number of weeks of eligibility for trade adjustment assistance depended on a combination of age and length of service in the firm or, ideally, in the U.S. labor force, as is the procedure in the labor protective arrangement made at the founding of Amtrak. An equitable scheme might allow a worker to receive benefits for each year of experience up to a maximum of five years, less one-half of the difference between his age and sixty. Every worker, however, would receive fifty-two weeks of benefits and none would receive benefits after reaching retirement age (sixty-five). Thus workers between the ages of fifty-two and sixty, with five years or more of work experience, could receive one to five years of benefits, and those over sixty a full five years of benefits. In addition, older workers could be given special treatment, such as early eligibility for medicare and social security benefits.

8. The Studebaker adjustment program is described on pp. 79–82.

9. Harold L. Sheppard, Louis A. Ferman, and Seymour Faber, *Too Old to Work—Too Young to Retire: A Case Study of a Permanent Plant Shutdown,* prepared for the Senate Special Committee on Unemployment Problems (GPO, 1960), p. 3.

10. George P. Shultz and Arnold R. Weber, *Strategies for the Displaced Worker* (Harper and Row, 1966), p. 7.

11. See, Sheppard, Ferman, and Faber, *Too Old to Work,* p. 19; William Haber, Louis A. Ferman, and James R. Hudson, *The Impact of Technological Change* (W. E. Upjohn Institute for Employment Research, 1963), pp. 13–14; and Richard C. Wilcock and Walter H. Franke, *Unwanted Workers* (London: Free Press of Glencoe, 1963), pp. 144–45.

Assistance for Communities

An important innovation in the Trade Act of 1974 is a program of adjustment assistance for communities. Partly because of the success and popularity in Congress of the Defense Department's program of assistance for communities and the good experience with an ad hoc program in South Bend, Indiana, in 1964, Congress has tended to view community-oriented programs favorably. Also, community-oriented programs are politically appealing because they may have an impact on a congressman's constituency.

A community is eligible for adjustment assistance if a significant number or proportion of workers in the area are wholly or partially separated from their jobs, if sales or production of firms in the area have declined, and if increased imports have "contributed importantly" to the separations. In other words, if one or more firms in an area are eligible for assistance and a significant number of workers has been affected, the community is eligible. It may also be eligible for assistance if firms desert the community to relocate their facilities in a foreign country and a significant number or proportion of workers is affected.

Under the program, petitions for assistance may be filed by local government entities. After an area is declared eligible, a trade-impacted-area council for adjustment assistance is established. The secretary of commerce, who administers the program, can send representatives to help in establishing the council, which must develop a proposal for an adjustment assistance plan. The secretary also may authorize grants to the council for professional and clerical staff.

The secretary must rule on the council's plan within sixty days of its submission. If he accepts it, two types of benefits are available. First, local authorities in the area are eligible to receive technical assistance and direct grants for acquiring and developing land and improving public works and public services. Second, private borrowers may receive special loan guarantees for funds to acquire, construct, modernize, or convert plants, and for working capital to finance activities aimed at bringing new job opportunities into the trade-impacted area. The community adjustment assistance program is supported by a specific congressional appropriation of funds: $100 million in expenditures was authorized for fiscal 1975 as part of the 1974 act.

Encouraging Workers to Move

Because the Trade Expansion Act did little to encourage the transfer of workers into more competitive industries, a number of means of remedying this deficiency were included in the Trade Act of 1974. The procedure for determining eligibility was streamlined, with full authority vested in the secretary of labor. Earlier, the training provisions were rarely used, partly because of the long delays in receiving benefits. A separate trust fund, derived from customs revenues, for training programs for trade-impacted workers gives the secretary of labor flexibility in providing training. Under the 1962 act, Labor Department funds tended to be fully committed to ongoing training and manpower programs and could not easily be diverted to assist trade-impacted workers.

The 1974 act also increases direct benefits for workers. The per diem and transportation allowances of those who must travel away from home to receive training have been increased. Workers who are not heads of households are now eligible for relocation allowances, whereas only heads of households formerly were. The speed up in determinations should also make the relocation allowances more attractive. A new type of allowance—a job search allowance—has been added to encourage mobility. A trade-impacted worker may be reimbursed up to $500 for 80 percent of necessary job search expenses, such as travel to another town in search of a job.

Many problems that must be overcome in attempting to make workers' movement away from trade-impacted areas less disruptive have not been adequately resolved. For example, the manner in which workers' benefits are given may actually discourage their moving. Workers' incentive to find new jobs diminishes as the financial support they receive approaches their previous income levels.[12] This problem is especially acute because worker benefits are now equal to 70 percent of former pay.

Some of the disincentive attendant to high levels of worker compensation might be removed by the use of lump-sum payments. The most generous application of this approach would allow a worker to receive the full fifty-two weeks of benefits as a lump sum without forfeiting any

12. See Martin S. Feldstein, *Lowering the Permanent Rate of Unemployment*, study prepared for the Joint Economic Committee of Congress (GPO, 1973), pp. 41–50.

of this if he found a job. A more modest application would allow him partial payment—say, the first thirteen weeks of his adjustment assistance benefits—as a lump sum; he would be eligible for the weekly allowance in subsequent weeks only if he had not yet found a job.

Another major problem in encouraging workers to move to better jobs is their fear of being unable to sell their houses at a price that would enable them to purchase comparable homes in a new location. Under the Defense Department's program for economic adjustment (described in chapter 6), department workers are protected against a capital loss on the sale of their homes. In England, there is a similar program to assist workers in moving out of depressed areas. Such provisions could be a distinct asset in a trade adjustment assistance program.

Early Warning and Timely Delivery of Benefits

Under the Trade Expansion Act of 1962 a great deal of time passed between the filing of a petition for adjustment assistance and the actual receipt of benefits by workers and firms. A determination first had to be made by the Tariff Commission, after which the secretary of labor or of commerce would certify the eligibility of individual workers or of firms. The cumbersome procedure has been shortened considerably, with determinations of eligibility for workers made directly by the secretary of labor and for firms directly by the secretary of commerce. The secretaries are given only sixty days to make their determinations. Furthermore, when an industry submits a petition for escape clause relief, the secretary of labor must be notified, and he is required to investigate the possibilities for adjustment assistance to the affected industry.

The Trade Act of 1974 requires, furthermore, that the secretaries of labor and commerce operate a system for monitoring data on production, consumption, and employment in industries producing items that are competitive with imports, and that they provide a summary of that information to Congress. Such a system can help to predict when an industry is heading for difficulty. The administrative machinery can thus be made ready to deliver benefits, and firms and workers can be alerted to apply for adjustment assistance. As yet another means of promoting "the efficient and effective delivery" of benefits, Congress established an interdepartmental adjustment assistance coordinating committee.[13]

13. 88 Stat. 2040

A Two-Tier System of Assistance

The Trade Act of 1974 provides eligibility for the full range of adjustment assistance benefits to firms and workers who qualify under the act. But the mobility of labor and the delivery of benefits could be improved if some benefits were made available early—well before serious dislocation occurs—while other benefits were reserved for more acute problems of dislocation. Thus the act could be improved by the institution of a two-tier system of adjustment assistance.[14] Benefits in the first tier would be available to whole industries adversely affected by trade.[15] To be eligible, an industry would have to have suffered a decline in sales or output and a decline in employment, and competitive imports would have to have increased appreciably, either relatively or absolutely, or exports would have to have declined.

A determination that an industry was adversely affected by trade would bring immediately into play a range of general adjustment assistance measures, for which all workers and firms in the industry would be automatically eligible. For example, workers might be made eligible for retraining, job placement, and relocation benefits. This would encourage workers to move out of sluggish industries into more dynamic and growing industries in which the demand for labor, particularly for skilled labor, might also be growing. The workers in the most adversely affected firms in a trade-impacted industry might be the least retrainable, because they are often older and less educated than workers in more viable firms within the industry. Retraining younger, more educated workers, enabling them to move out of the industry, might make room for reabsorption into the industry of the less trainable workers who are adversely affected.

14. For a description of the two-tier approach, see National Association of Manufacturers, "Trade Adjustment Assistance," pp. 52–55.

15. The definition of an industry is particularly important. If the category of products is defined too broadly, too many different types of firms would be covered, some of whom were never subject to import competition and thus should not be eligible for adjustment assistance. It is not easy to specify an ideal industry categorization. The standard nomenclature, or Tariff Schedule of the United States (TSUS) categorization, contains too many different commodities—about 7,000. Furthermore, it is not possible to obtain domestic production figures for each TSUS category, so the criterion would be impossible to apply. The standard industrial classification (SIC) provides a better basis for obtaining data on production or shipments by industry. The import and export classifications, however, are not easily matched to SIC categories.

For all firms in an adversely affected industry the first tier of benefits would include immediate eligibility for technical assistance. Furthermore, all firms could be required to give advance notice of terminations of workers' jobs or plant shutdowns, which would enable the Department of Labor to prepare immediately for delivery of adjustment assistance benefits to workers. Once an industry was declared adversely affected by trade, the Departments of Labor and Commerce could notify all firms and organized worker groups in the industry that they were automatically eligible for the first tier of adjustment assistance benefits and that they could apply for a second tier of benefits. The departments could assist workers and firms in preparing petitions for this second tier.

The second tier of benefits for workers would include mainly trade readjustment allowances for those whose firms had suffered a decline in output or sales and a significant decline in employment. For firms, the second tier would include loans and loan guarantees for specific adjustment projects. All firms in the industry would be eligible to apply for benefits, and their applications would be judged solely on the merits of the project. Only the industry as a whole, not the firm, would need to show a decline in output or sales.

Applications for loans and loan guarantees would be judged on the basis of the commercial viability of the proposed project and on whether the proposal had adequately taken into account the interests of the firm's workers. Assistance to firms would be directed to those well-run firms that nevertheless might not have sufficient access to private capital markets on favorable terms. There would be no bailing-out operations for the benefit of firms with poor prospects.

Conclusions

The trade reform bill presented to Congress in early 1973 virtually emasculated the adjustment assistance program. The administration argued that the old program had been a failure and that there was no way to design an effective program at reasonable cost. Thus, its bill eliminated the programs of adjustment assistance to firms and substantially reduced benefits for most workers. The administration argued that the way to help unemployed workers was not through adjustment assistance but through reform of the state-federal system of unemployment insurance.

The House and Ways and Means Committee and the Senate Finance

Committee rewrote the adjustment assistance provisions of the act. The result is a legislative program that is an improvement over the 1962 Trade Expansion Act. The vitality of the program, however, depends very much on its administration. The secretaries of labor and commerce have broad responsibilities, as well as great flexibility in administering the program. The strength of the new program for communities, in particular, depends on the priority and visibility given it by the secretary of commerce. Successful community programs require high-level attention and concern within the government; the administration now has far more effective tools than were available in the past.

The adjustment assistance program for communities was almost entirely a creation of the Senate Finance Committee. Streamlining the administration of benefits for workers and restoring the program for firms were important contributions of the House Ways and Means Committee. Both committees added a number of provisions that increased the potential impact of adjustment assistance on worker mobility.

To be sure, the trade act can be improved. The benefits of an industry approach to an adjustment assistance program seem particularly large. Other, easier reforms can also help the trade program. The disincentive to search for a new job that trade readjustment allowances create could be mitigated. There could be a stronger emphasis on the problem of the older worker. And eligibility could be extended to firms indirectly affected by trade and to workers who lose their jobs because their plants are moved to other countries. But the overall program of adjustment aid has been greatly improved in the 1974 act. Nearly twice as much was expended on worker assistance in the first eighteen months of the 1974 act as in the thirteen years of the 1962 act—about $141 million versus $86 million.

Further improvements in assistance might very well be made through a different approach—a broad adjustment assistance program designed to assist not only the victims of dislocation caused by changing patterns of international trade but also those who suffer from economic dislocation generally, whatever the cause. Adjustment assistance efforts in the United States, and in other countries, that are not related to the adverse impact of foreign trade have taken many forms—aid to communities, aid to workers, aid to industries. Some of these approaches have been applied to trade adjustment assistance. These programs, which are discussed in chapters 6–9, could form the nucleus of a broad U.S. policy of adjustment assistance aimed at the entire range of causes of dislocation.

CHAPTER SIX

Aid to Communities and Regions

A NUMBER of adjustment assistance programs in recent years have had a regional or a community focus. The Defense Department has operated a continuing program to facilitate adjustment to closings of military facilities or cutbacks in military and aerospace contracts in communities of varying sizes all over the United States. An ad hoc program of assistance to South Bend, Indiana, initiated by President Johnson in 1964 when a large Studebaker plant shut down, was designed to help a severely disrupted local economy. General programs, not dependent on a specific cause of dislocation, have been administered by the Appalachian Regional Commission and the Economic Development Administration of the Department of Commerce to aid whole regions with chronic employment problems.

The Defense Department's Economic Adjustment Program

Because the Defense Department has had to be concerned with the effect of its activities on local economies, particularly since World War II, an Office of Economic Adjustment (OEA) was created in the department in the early sixties. At first the office worked informally, coordinating the programs of economic assistance offered by the Departments of Labor, Commerce, Health, Education, and Welfare, and Housing and Urban

Development, the Small Business Administration, the Office of Economic Opportunity, and other federal agencies. It originally dealt mostly with problems brought on by the closing of military bases. In March 1970, however, a cabinet-level Interagency Economic Adjustment Committee was established by presidential charter and the Office of Economic Adjustment, still in the Defense Department, was chosen to act as the committee's staff. Since then, both the committee and the office have had a more aggressive role in planning and assistance for defense-impacted areas. They not only offer help to communities affected by base closings, major reductions in defense personnel forces, and cutbacks in defense contracts, but have also become involved in planning assistance programs in several areas impacted by reductions in aerospace programs. In fact, since the late sixties, base closures have become a less and less important concern, and defense contract cutbacks and reductions in military hiring have become the main causes of dislocation.

In 1968, according to Department of Defense estimates, about 8 million jobs, of which 4.5 million were civilian, could be related directly to defense expenditures. By 1974, the number of civilian jobs attributable to defense expenditures had declined by about 1.8 million and total employment in defense-related jobs by about 3.2 million (see table 6-1). The April 1973 announcement by the Department of Defense of 274 actions to "consolidate, reduce, realign, or close" military installations had an effect that was typical of such announcements: some 42,800 civilian and military jobs were eliminated. Approximately that number of jobs was lost each year in base closings in 1961, 1963, 1964, 1965, 1967, 1969, and 1970.[1]

The losses were distributed unevenly. In the early seventies, California, Texas, and New England were badly hit. In San Francisco, for example, approximately 5,000 jobs were lost with the closing of Hunter's Point Naval Shipyard, the city's largest single industrial employer. The closing of Laredo Air Force Base, Texas, in September 1973 dislocated 700 employees in an area where the annual unemployment rate ranged between 10 percent and 12 percent. Realignments[2] at three installations in Rhode

1. National Council for Urban Economic Development, "Community Economic Adjustment to Defense Cutbacks" (report of a seminar held by the council, April 25–26, 1974; processed), p. 5.

2. The Defense Department considers a "realignment" to be any action that affects the distribution or use of department personnel and resources. The realign-

Table 6-1. *Employment Attributable to Defense Expenditures, 1965 and 1968–76*[a]

Millions of employees

Defense employment	*1965*	*1968*	*1969*	*1970*	*1971*	*1972*	*1973*	*1974*	*1975*[b]	*1976*[b]
Total	5.8	8.0	7.7	6.6	5.8	5.3	5.0	4.8	4.6	4.6
Civilian	3.1	4.5	4.2	3.6	3.1	3.0	2.7	2.7	2.5	2.5
Public	1.0	1.3	1.3	1.2	1.1	1.1	1.0	1.0	1.0	1.0
Private	2.1	3.2	2.9	2.4	2.0	1.9	1.7	1.7	1.5	1.5
Military	2.7	3.5	3.5	3.0	2.7	2.3	2.3	2.1	2.1	2.1

Source: U.S. Department of Defense, Office of Assistant Secretary of Defense (Comptroller), "Program Budget, Plans and Systems," internal data package, table 4-1 ([1975]; processed).

a. Strength at the end of the fiscal year.

b. Preliminary estimates.

Island affected 5,000 civilian and 17,000 military positions, creating an adverse economic impact throughout the state. And in the Boston area, Defense Department actions displaced about 6,000 workers, 5,500 of whom were employed at the shipyard.

Such communities have been provided assistance by the Office of Economic Adjustment, but the office has usually acted only in response to a request for assistance. Most often such requests are made through a member of Congress. The OEA is willing to take action only when the community has been highly reliant on defense expenditures—as a rule of thumb, if at least 2 percent of its work force has been in defense-related employment.

Furthermore, the OEA has taken the initiative only in coordinating the readjustment activities. It has relied heavily on personnel and funds from other government agencies; more important, it has stressed local community action, including improvement of local planning, changes in real estate zoning regulations, and the setting up of institutions designed to attract private investment to the impacted area. Most of the jobs that have been developed stem from private investment activities rather than direct government expenditures.

Several kinds of assistance have been provided to communities. Technical assistance, to help a community devise a development plan, is offered by a small OEA staff of planning experts. They visit the community to talk with community leaders and help them plan a development strategy. Usually, technical experts from various federal departments and agencies, often from regional offices, accompany them. The plans spell out specific actions to be taken by various elements of the community and by state and federal government agencies.

The fact that a written plan exists has usually proved helpful in tapping resources from ongoing federal programs. The OEA has helped communities secure aid from a wide variety of federal agencies. For example, the Manpower Office of the Department of Labor has made grants for job development and training. The Economic Development Administration of the Department of Commerce has frequently been involved—making planning grants, providing loans for extension of sewer and water facilities to an industrial park area, helping to set up an area development corpora-

---

ments of particular concern to the Office of Economic Adjustment include those having an adverse effect on employment, and may include base closures, major layoffs, and terminations of or cutbacks in contracts with private enterprises.

tion. The Department of Transportation has helped in planning road development and stepping up road construction activity. The Department of Housing and Urban Development has provided planning grants and loans for construction of housing, sewers, and water systems. The Department of Agriculture has conducted a market study for Wichita, Kansas, and organized a marketing study for a cold storage facility for San Joaquin County, California.

When the Department of Defense decides to close a military base, the community is given the opportunity to obtain any of the property that is surplus to the needs of the federal government. Surplus federal property often offers the locality a chance to expand community services and improve the economic base of the community. The community is required to purchase both land and buildings at fair market value, although the value may be reduced if the property is to be used for certain educational, recreational, or health care services. The plan the community has developed, frequently with OEA's assistance, for reuse of the property is thus very important.

The Defense Department holds up its help in Wichita, Kansas, as a model of successful community assistance planning. Recovery from sharp curtailments in defense and aerospace activity in Wichita was rapid—the rate of unemployment dropped from the 11.6 percent high it reached in June 1971 to 4.7 percent in April 1972, and average employment increased by 18,650 between 1971 and 1973.[3] Wichita began experiencing a construction and investment boom, and substantial government investment went into the area. Contributions to the rehabilitation effort included a Department of Labor grant of $8 million for job development programs; the Economic Development Administration's approval of grants of $1.8 million for utility improvements in an industrial park, $1.5 million for improved water supply, and $0.3 million for a Civil Defense Center; a Housing and Urban Development grant of $1.3 million for renovation of the water system and $0.5 million for construction of a neighborhood training and recreation facility; release of $12 million of impounded federal highway funds in the area; and approval of a new Naval Reserve Center, costing $650,000.[4]

In addition to helping communities, the Department of Defense has

3. Data provided by the Kansas State Employment Service (August 1975).

4. See President's Committee, "Opportunities for a Community in Economic Distress."

made special efforts to aid its own employees adversely affected by defense cutbacks. When possible, they are offered defense jobs in other locations. For the ten years ending in 1974, however, about 250,000 Defense Department personnel lost their jobs. About 23 percent of these former employees resigned or retired, but about 81 percent of the remainder were placed in new jobs through the department's nationwide computerized system that matches jobs and skills.[5] In areas of the country that are hit especially hard, the department sets up a special regional referral and placement system to strengthen efforts to assist affected personnel.

Both military and civilian employees of the Defense Department who have had to relocate because of base closures or reductions in employment have been given financial assistance to compensate for losses incurred in selling their homes. Through June 30, 1975, 3,807 homeowners had been compensated a total of $5.5 million for declines in the market value of their homes because of base closures; 2,344 homes had been acquired under the homeowners' assistance program of the Federal Housing Administration for a total of $14.1 million; 1,849 mortgages, worth $18.8 million, had been assumed; and mortgage holders had received a total of $3.2 million in FHA mortgage insurance payments on foreclosures.[6]

Between 1961 and 1975, more than two hundred communities were assisted by the Office of Economic Adjustment. Between January 1969 and January 1973 alone, seventy-one communities in thirty-four states and Puerto Rico received help. In thirty-six of these communities, where the Defense Department feels that adjustment plans have been fully implemented, about 79,000 jobs were lost due to defense cutbacks and 85,000 new nondefense jobs were created in implementing the plans. Realignments announced in April 1973 were expected to result in 33,000 job losses by 1976;[7] by January 1974, however, 12,700 of these workers had already been placed in jobs, and 4,000 new jobs had been created.

In many of the communities adjustment was rapid. Substantial new

5. Unpublished data provided by the U.S. Department of Defense, Office of Economic Adjustment (July 1975).

6. U.S. Department of Defense, Office of the Deputy Assistant Secretary (Installation and Logistics), Installations and Housing, "Homeowners Assistance Program" (March 31, 1975; processed), p. 1.

7. This figure includes only workers in 27 communities that requested assistance from the OEA. The 274 actions taken in April 1973 were expected to put a total of 42,800 people out of work.

private investment as well as government funds flowed into affected areas such as Wichita; Rockford, Illinois; and Sherman and Dennison, Texas. Members of Congress from these areas and their staff and local community leaders indicate that the Office of Economic Adjustment was of substantial help, and the office seems to have a favorable image in many affected communities.

It could be argued that there has been no net gain in jobs since much of the new investment brought into impacted areas would otherwise have taken place in other regions. On the other hand, it is better that industry locate in high unemployment areas than that workers be forced to move to new locations to find jobs. It is also desirable that investment resources flow into defense-impacted areas with idle labor resources and underutilized economic infrastructures. This is a natural part of the adjustment process. Furthermore, it is just as likely that the new private investment in such areas represents, at least in part, additional investment that occurs because of a general increase in profitable investment opportunities.

Although the Office of Economic Adjustment is a small bureau with little more to offer than the services of its professional staff of about twenty experts, it has pursued a seemingly successful program of economic adjustment assistance. Part of the success must be attributed to the high-level priority given to the problem. The presidential charter to the Interagency Committee and its cabinet-level status helped to bring about the maximum degree of cooperation and effort by the federal departments and agencies involved in assistance programs. Their responsiveness and flexibility, on which the Office of Economic Adjustment relies, have been diminished, however, since the changeover from direct federal funding of local projects to decentralized block grants.

Another factor in the success of the program has probably been the large amount of administrative flexibility given to the Office of Economic Adjustment—it has not done its work under legislative authorization. Rather, the office has used self-imposed guidelines to decide which communities to assist. The factors most important in the decision to provide help have been the need for assistance and the willingness of the community to cooperate.

One serious problem for the program is the lack of advance warning of base closures and cutbacks. Because the political repercussions that follow the announcement of defense expenditure realignments are felt at every governmental level, the formal announcements are made on the latest possible date even though the realignment decisions have been made well in advance. If the information were made known to the community at an earlier time, more comprehensive, long-term planning by local leaders might take place.[8]

Another problem faced by the Defense Department's program is the numerous restrictions placed on the use of federal property by existing law and the difficulties faced by communities in acquiring such property at less than fair market value.

Despite these problems, the program has been highly successful in providing adjustment assistance to communities adversely affected by defense or aerospace cutbacks. It has helped quite a number of communities over a long period of time. It provides a useful model for community adjustment assistance efforts that might be applied to communities adversely affected by changing patterns of international trade. In fact, some of the communities assisted under the Defense Department program have also been impacted by trade. In such communities, a number of firms and workers have benefited from trade adjustment assistance at the same time the community was receiving assistance from the Defense Department for defense-related reasons.

The Studebaker Adjustment Program

On December 10, 1963, the Studebaker Corporation announced that it was abandoning production at South Bend, Indiana, and opening a plant in Hamilton, Ontario. The Studebaker Corporation was in financial difficulty at the time and the management felt that the corporation's passenger car production could survive only if it were moved to Canada. Canadian wages, which were a little more than 70 percent of U.S. wages, and the devalued Canadian dollar made Canadian production financially attractive.

Studebaker production facilities had been located in South Bend for over sixty-one years, and in September 1963 employed nearly 8,700 people, or about 10 percent of the labor force of St. Joseph County. Soon

8. National Council for Urban Economic Development, "Community Economic Adjustment to Defense Cutbacks," p. 3.

after the closing of the plant, many management and skilled workers left the city, but most of the labor force did not, and the unemployment rate jumped from 2.4 percent to over 9 percent in a four-month period.[9] Many of the severed workers had firmly implanted roots in the South Bend area—68 percent owned homes there. Families with three generations of Studebaker workers were not uncommon.

Many of the workers were old—65 percent were over forty-five and half were over fifty—and, as a sample survey taken four months after the closing revealed, they had by far the most difficulty in finding jobs.[10] The average worker had twenty years' seniority at the time of closing, and many had never had to apply for another job. Their union had no agreement with Studebaker on severance pay for hourly workers, and it was estimated that the union's supplementary unemployment benefits fund would last no more than a week. All of the workers were eligible for unemployment insurance benefits, but very few were eligible for the maximum weekly payment of $36 and the maximum period of twenty-six weeks because of previous periods of unemployment before Studebaker abandoned its plant.[11] Most workers, however, received extended payments of $20 to $25 for fifteen to twenty weeks through a federal emergency fund authorized by President Johnson. Those who were sixty years old or older received their full pension rights, but because the pension fund was barely adequate to provide full vesting for them, those left received less than 15 percent of their partially vested rights.[12]

The announcement of the Studebaker closing created a crisis atmosphere in South Bend. John Brademas, the congressman from the area, urged President Johnson to mobilize federal resources. The President, the secretaries of labor and commerce, and Brademas went to South Bend to highlight their concern. President Johnson appointed an interagency committee to mobilize resources at all levels and cut bureaucratic red tape. The committee's meetings, held in the area, were attended by Congressman Brademas and Senators Birch Bayh and Vance Hartke, representatives from the United Auto Workers and from Studebaker, local business

9. J. John Palen and Frank J. Fahey, "Unemployment and Reemployment Success: An Analysis of the Studebaker Shutdown," *Industrial and Labor Relations Review*, vol. 21 (January 1968), p. 235.

10. Ibid., pp. 237–40.

11. Area Redevelopment Administration, *Closing of the Studebaker Plant: South Bend, Indiana*, ARA casebook 5 (Government Printing Office, 1964), p. 4.

12. Speech by Congressman John Brademas, Feb. 26, 1974.

and government leaders, and representatives from private organizations such as the United Community Services of St. Joseph County and Notre Dame University.

The adjustment plan took many forms. Training programs under the Manpower Development and Training Act that were already in existence in South Bend were greatly expanded. Project ABLE (ability based on long experience), which was a joint venture of the Department of Labor's Office of Manpower, Automation, and Training and the National Council of the Aging, was organized after the shutdown to retrain workers over fifty years of age and find them jobs. Studebaker provided its facilities free of charge to house some of the training programs. Community agencies were mobilized to search for job opportunities and attempt to break down employer resistance to hiring older workers. The Labor Department sent specialists to South Bend who, through the United States and state employment services, initiated a program of broad personal services to the workers and helped speed up the delivery of unemployment insurance benefits. About forty men from the United Auto Workers and the industrial relations staff of Studebaker were sent to counsel workers about training opportunities and new employment. Without this counseling, it was highly unlikely that workers would have accepted retraining. They were apprehensive about taking and failing tests required for new positions, so the retraining process included dummy tests to familiarize the men with stumbling blocks of this kind. Almost 70 percent of the 1,300 men who received retraining in a variety of trades finished their courses. Out of those graduates, 70 percent found jobs almost immediately.[13] Some workers were assisted in relocating in other areas where jobs were available. Moving subsidies were provided under the Manpower Development and Training Act. Surplus food was distributed to more than 2,800 individuals in families of former Studebaker workers under a special federal program. Late payments were permitted on federal housing, veterans', and small business loans, and satisfactory arrangements were made for a local bank to take over management of the former employees' credit union.

Special efforts were made to attract new industry to the area. A mayor's commission organized to look for new industry had the help of local business leaders, Studebaker, labor leaders, and government officials at the federal, state, and local levels. The Department of Labor reclassified the

13. Robert A. Wright, *New York Times,* Nov. 14, 1966.

area so that it would receive preference in federal government procurement contracts. Congressman Brademas organized a government procurement conference in early March 1964. Representatives from the Army, Navy, Air Force, and six civilian agencies met with corporate officials to discuss contracts currently open for bidding worth $100 million. As a result, 339 firms were added to federal agencies' bidders' lists, and the Defense Department alone received 300 sets of bids from attending companies.[14]

Much of the assistance effort was directed at finding new firms to move into the abandoned Studebaker facilities. A Defense Department contract for military trucks held by Studebaker was switched to Kaiser Jeep, which moved into part of the Studebaker plant and employed 400 workers. Other large firms bought or leased parts of the plant attractively priced by the corporation. By May 1966 fourteen firms, including Allied Products Corporation, Cummins Engine Company, and Hutchins Tool and Die, were housed in the Studebaker facilities, employing almost 4,000 workers.[15]

Adjustment to the Studebaker closing in South Bend was rapid and aided by a growing economy. Many of the firms already located in the area expanded employment, thus easing the sudden slack. By October 1965 the unemployment rate in St. Joseph County had diminished to 2.1 percent, which was lower than the rate before the closing of the plant.[16] The success of the program can be attributed partly to the active interest of Congressman Brademas and President Johnson. A fortuitous factor was the fact that federal manpower training programs were just beginning to expand and there was a great deal of enthusiastic support by manpower administrators anxious to test new programs.

Aid to Depressed Regions

In addition to assistance to specific communities, there are a number of broadly based regional approaches to economic adjustment problems, such as those administered by regional commissions and the Economic Development Administration.

Declining industries are often concentrated in specific regions. For

14. ARA, *Closing of the Studebaker Plant,* p. 13.

15. News Media Memorandum, South Bend-Mishawaka Chamber of Commerce, May 20, 1966.

16. ARA, *Closing of the Studebaker Plant,* p. 4.

example, about thirty years ago, 10 percent of the work force in the Appalachian region worked in coal mines. By 1960, employment in the mines had dropped from about 500,000 to less than 200,000, or only about 3.5 percent of the Appalachian work force. Between 1950 and 1960, employment on the railroads dropped 40 percent in Appalachia due to the shift from trains to trucks and to improvements in railroad technology.[17] When a region becomes depressed due to changing economic patterns, it is extremely difficult for displaced workers to find new jobs, in contrast to workers who lose jobs in dynamic and growing areas. Government programs aimed at specific depressed regions can help the workers to relocate in other areas or they can attempt to bring new industry into the region.

In the late 1950s several bills were introduced into Congress to aid depressed areas, but all either failed to pass or were vetoed by President Eisenhower. Finally, on May 1, 1961, President Kennedy signed the Area Redevelopment Act (ARA). The administering agency was the newly formed Area Redevelopment Administration of the Department of Commerce. The act authorized $389 million to be spent in more than a thousand depressed counties or similar areas including more than a fifth of the total U.S. population.[18] In order to qualify for assistance, a depressed area was required to form a redevelopment corporation representing various community interest groups, and submit an overall economic development program. These programs were to be helpful to the regions in attracting not only ARA funds but other federal grants and loans. Less than 50 percent of the eligible areas in the first year, and 20 percent of those remaining in the second year, qualified.[19]

In February 1962, President Kennedy introduced another bill aimed at depressed regions, the Accelerated Public Works Act (APWA). The program provided $900 million in grants for up to 75 percent of the cost of public works projects. Communities eligible for ARA assistance were also eligible for these funds, but the new program extended to an additional 150 communities, with a population of 22 million. The program was placed under ARA jurisdiction in the Department of Commerce.[20]

17. U.S. Economic Development Administration, "Regional Economic Development in the United States" (October 1967; processed), p. VII-5.

18. Sar Levitan, *Federal Aid to Depressed Areas* (Johns Hopkins University Press, 1964), pp. 27 and 66.

19. Ibid., pp. 68–69.

20. Donald N. Rothblatt, *Regional Planning: The Appalachian Experience* (Heath, 1971), p. 42.

In March 1965 a special program for the Appalachian region was signed into law by President Johnson. This mountainous region in the eastern United States, which included all of West Virginia and parts of twelve other states, had been eligible for ARA and APWA funds, but Congress and the President felt a special program for Appalachia was justified. The region, larger than Italy, Austria, and Switzerland together, and with a population almost half as large as Canada's, was acutely depressed. In 1960 the unemployment rate was approximately 7.1 percent, whereas the national average was 5 percent. During the period 1950 to 1960, the net migration out of the area was estimated to be 2,450,000 persons.[21]

The passage of the Appalachian Regional Development Act of 1965 was preceded by several commission reports and appeals to Congress and the President by local Appalachian interests. As a direct result of a disastrous flood in eastern Kentucky in 1957, the governor appointed an Eastern Kentucky Regional Planning Commission. In January 1960 the commission issued a report that contained an institutional strategy for developing the entire Appalachian region. In May 1960 the governors of the Appalachian states met in Annapolis and later formed a Conference of Appalachian Governors (CAG). The staff of CAG prepared a report and recommendations which the governors presented to President Kennedy in May 1961. Their timing, however, was inauspicious, for the President had signed the more general Area Redevelopment Act only a week earlier. Another disaster, the Appalachian floods in the spring of 1963, triggered another appeal by the CAG. The President responded with the establishment of the President's Appalachian Regional Commission, which prepared a report forming the basis for the Appalachian Regional Development Act. The Appalachian Regional Commission was then reorganized and charged with the administration of the program.

Six months after passage of the Appalachian program, Congress passed the Public Works and Economic Development Act of 1965. This act greatly expanded the scope of the original ARA, set up an Economic Development Administration within the Department of Commerce to administer general regional development programs, and provided, under title five, for the institution of regional planning commissions similar to the Appalachian Regional Commission.

21. Ibid., p. 45.

The Appalachia Program

The Appalachian Regional Commission consists of the governors of the thirteen Appalachian states, a federal cochairman appointed by the President, and a representative appointed by the member states. The commission, served by a small staff headed by an executive director, is responsible for formulation and implementation of a comprehensive regional development plan. It approves specific projects and releases funds either to federal agencies or to state or local governments for implementing the projects. In addition, it makes "supplemental grants"—partially constrained block grants to state and local agencies, which may be used to increase the federal contribution to as much as 80 percent of the total cost for projects authorized under other federal programs.

Planning under the Appalachia program begins at both the top and the bottom levels. Sectoral allocations are determined largely by congressional appropriations to the Appalachian Regional Commission, whereas projects within the sectors, except for highway projects, are proposed by the individual states involved. In the early years of the commission, the emphasis was on highways—two-thirds of appropriations for the years 1965 through 1967 went for highways. The highway program, devoted largely to building limited-access, high-speed, interstate roads, was based largely on the recommendations of the 1964 report of the President's Appalachian Regional Commission. Between 1968 and 1973, however, emphasis shifted slightly away from highway development, while construction of access roads received increasing attention. Outside the highway sector the most important allocations have been supplemental grants for localities (37 percent of nonhighway appropriations through 1974), health care (29 percent), vocational education facilities (19 percent), and mine reclamation and fish and wildlife projects (6 percent).[22]

Nonhighway projects, including those dealing with access roads, are proposed by the states as part of an overall plan for the region. In formulating plans, the state govennments depend on local development districts—multicounty planning and administrative units designed to elicit local participation in the planning efforts and to strengthen local government contacts with state and federal agencies.

The Appalachian Regional Commission gradually adopted a policy of

22. Based on data in U.S. Appalachian Regional Commission, *1974 Annual Report of the Appalachian Regional Commission* (GPO, 1974), pp. 30–31.

insisting that states allocate their funds to areas of potential growth "where the return on public dollars invested will be greatest." By the end of fiscal 1968, those areas, comprising about 12 percent of the area of the Appalachian region, had received about 95 percent of the funds available for nonhighway projects.[23]

Through 1974, almost $2.3 billion had been appropriated for Appalachian programs, of which $1.35 billion was for highway development.[24] The emphasis of the commission has been on steady, long-term economic growth rather than any kind of crisis relief or temporary assistance, and in aggregate economic terms, conditions in the region have improved somewhat.[25] In 1962, the unemployment rate for the region was 8.7 percent, while the national average was 5.5 percent. By 1970 unemployment in Appalachia had dropped to 5.0 percent, compared with 4.9 percent for the nation as a whole. Per capita income in Appalachia grew slightly faster than in the nation at large and net migration out of the region in the decade of the sixties was only 1.1 million persons, compared to 2.2 million persons in the previous decade.[26] Though it is difficult to attribute these changes specifically to the Appalachia programs, the trend is encouraging.

The Economic Development Administration

The Public Works and Economic Development Act of 1965 was the result of an attempt to enlarge the scope of and correct some of the problems of implementing the Area Redevelopment Act. The act created the Economic Development Administration (EDA), which succeeded the Area Redevelopment Administration.

Eligibility for benefits under the act was given to areas that had unemployment rates above 6 percent, and 50 percent above the national average for three of the previous four years, 75 percent above the average for two of the previous three years, or 100 percent above the average for one of the previous two years, although other criteria could be used to make an area eligible. An area was defined as either a county, a multi-

23. Ibid., pp. 157–58.

24. Appalachian Regional Commission, *1974 Annual Report,* p. 27.

25. John H. Cumberland has praised the commission for its "innovations in cooperative federal-state-local planning for regional development" (*Regional Development Experiences and Prospects in the United States of America* [Paris: Mouton & Co., 1971], p. 102).

26. U.S. Appalachian Regional Commission, *1971 Annual Report of the Appalachian Regional Commission* (GPO, 1971), pp. 14–15.

county labor market area so defined by the Department of Labor, a municipality of 250,000 or more residents, or an Indian reservation.

For administrative reasons, areas are often combined into development districts, which form the basic units for the allocation of benefits. A development district must have a designated growth center which provides a focus for the grants and loans given under the act. In order to receive benefits, a district must have an approved development plan, which the EDA will help draw up.

Benefits to eligible areas take several forms. Grants may be made for up to 50 percent of the costs of public facilities such as industrial parks, roads, and utilities that can be expected to attract new industrial or commercial facilities into the areas. And supplemental grants are permitted that can be used to increase the amounts allocated for other federal grant-in-aid programs. Loans may be made for up to 100 percent of the cost of public works projects or up to 65 percent of the costs of private industrial or commercial projects. Government guarantees on up to 90 percent of the outstanding balance on working capital loans from private lending institutions are also available. The secretary of commerce is authorized to provide technical assistance both for projects and areas, and planning grants may be given to development district planning organizations. In addition to these operating programs, the EDA sponsors research on problems of depressed areas.

During the first ten months of its existence, the EDA certified 1,329 depressed areas for assistance; these areas, with an average unemployment rate of 7.6 percent, had a population of 50 million persons and covered about one-third of the nation's counties.[27] The number of areas eligible was more than double that under the old ARA. In subsequent years, however, a number of areas lost their eligibility, and the number of eligible areas fell to less than 1,000 in 1970.[28] In the early seventies, the number rose again and by the end of fiscal 1974 was almost 1,800.[29] By that time, a total of about $2.1 billion had been obligated by the EDA, of which $1.6 billion was for public works and $340 million for business loans.[30]

27. U.S. Economic Development Administration and Office of Regional Economic Development, *Building Communities with New Jobs: First Annual Report, Fiscal Year 1966* (GPO, 1967), pp. 7–9.

28. U.S. Economic Development Administration, *Jobs for America, Annual Report Fiscal 1970* (GPO, 1971), pp. 8–9.

29. U.S. Economic Development Administration, *1974 Annual Report* (GPO, 1975), p. 2.

30. Ibid., p. 87.

The EDA adopted a policy of allocating funds first to the areas that were most depressed. Since the worst areas are often those with the least potential, this policy is unlikely to lead to a successful rescue effort.

In a 1970 evaluation of EDA's programs,[31] made in terms of the dollar amount of grants and loans per job created, the program appeared to have been reasonably successful. However, the ratio used as an indicator is suspect because it depends on estimates of jobs created directly and indirectly, which are technically difficult measurements to make. The fact that the expenditures-per-job-created ratio is relatively low does not foreclose the possibility that the ratio could have been even lower if some other program had been implemented instead. It is even possible that jobs have been created by the EDA program at the expense of jobs in more affluent and dynamic areas not covered by the EDA.

Under title five of the 1965 act, multistate development regions were created along the model of the Appalachian Regional Commission. By 1973, seven such regional commissions had been created—for the Ozarks, the Pacific Northwest, New England, the Upper Great Lakes, the Eastern Coastal Plains, Four Corners (an area including Arizona, Colorado, New Mexico, and Utah), and the Old West (a region between Minnesota and the Pacific Northwest). Most of the country is now covered by the act and the regions have thus lost some of their special significance, but they do provide for a regional planning mechanism. The new commissions, however, do not yet have the powers or capabilities of the Appalachian Regional Commission since they do not control large amounts of funds and are thus not able to enforce their planning goals on the regions; they have received funds from the secretary of commerce only for technical assistance, research activities, and planning grants.

Conclusions

The assistance programs of the Economic Development Administration and the Appalachian Regional Commission have emphasized "place" rather than people. Most assistance has gone to state and local governments and business firms, because the basic thrust of these programs is to

31. See U.S. Economic Development Administration, *The Economic Development Administration's Public Works Program: An Evaluation,* vol. 1, *Summary of Findings and Survey Methodology* (GPO, 1970).

bring industry to the workers rather than relocate workers. Little emphasis is placed on training and education within EDA, and the EDA's programs are only modestly coordinated with the manpower development and training efforts of the Department of Labor. The emphasis on place reflects the desire of congressmen to protect the population base and economic viability of their own areas. The original legislative proposal for aid to depressed areas, made by Senator Paul Douglas in the early sixties, included programs for retraining and relocation of workers, but the legislation that subsequently passed Congress shifted the emphasis away from manpower development. In contrast, the efforts to help South Bend, Indiana, recover from the shock of the closing of the Studebaker plant were focused largely on manpower training, especially for older workers.

The Economic Development Administration's programs have been the least successful of the assistance efforts. Their main weakness has been their tendency to spread resources very thinly over a wide area and, when funds have been concentrated, to allocate to the poorest areas rather than to communities with the greatest potential for recovery. The attempts to aid South Bend and the Defense Department's program have been widely praised as successful efforts to provide impetus for community and regional development and provide better models for assistance to trade-impacted communities. These programs have generated more action and visible progress for a number of reasons. They are crisis oriented and have operated in an atmosphere of urgency and acute need. They have captured the interest of local politicians and community leaders and have built upon and utilized community pride. They also have attracted high-level, executive-branch concern and leadership.

CHAPTER SEVEN

Helping Workers Adjust

RESISTANCE to economic change may be greatly reduced if the dislocating effects of change on workers can be minimized. For example, manpower training and counseling services can make the transition between jobs less traumatic, various benefits and allowances can make it less costly, and transfer rights and good placement services can make it less time-consuming. This chapter considers means of improving worker adjustment, including manpower training, income maintenance, and measures found specifically in collective bargaining agreements.

The effectiveness of such programs is crucial to the issue of trade adjustment assistance, since only the fact, and not the cause, of dislocation is of any real importance to the worker. Current worker adjustment measures may be adequate for helping trade-impacted workers; where they are not, special provisions may have to be made for such workers.

Manpower Training

One approach to the problem of worker adjustment to economic change is training workers to acquire new skills as technological change, market forces, and government policies shift the nature of production and the demand for labor skills. For many years, private employers have conducted training programs for their workers and have helped to pay their tuition for job-related schooling.[1]

1. See U.S. Bureau of Labor Statistics (BLS), *Major Collective Bargaining Agreements: Training and Retraining Provisions,* bulletin 1425-7 (Government Printing Office, 1969), p. 1.

In the early sixties, federal, state, and local governments began to enter the field of worker training. The Area Redevelopment Act of 1961, for example, contained training provisions for workers. Full-scale federal involvement began in 1962, with the Manpower Development and Training Act (MDTA). One of the largest of the federal programs, it enrolled 2.1 million trainees at a cost of $3.2 billion between 1963 and 1973.[2] It provided for both classroom and on-the-job training. After 1966, the program was amended to require that at least 65 percent of the enrollees be disadvantaged (that is, from an ethnic minority, physically handicapped, or under twenty-one or over forty-five years of age).

The manpower provisions of the Economic Opportunity Act of 1964 created more than a dozen national manpower programs, among them the Neighborhood Youth Corps (NYC), the Job Corps, Job Opportunities in the Business Sector (JOBS), and the Work Incentive (WIN) program. These programs, operated on direct grants and contracts with public and private organizations, were handled by the Department of Labor. The Youth Corps between 1965 and 1973 provided part-time and summer employment and training for 4.95 million school dropouts, with federal expenditures totaling $3.1 billion.[3] The Job Corps began in 1970 to provide remedial education, training, and counseling services for disadvantaged youths sixteen to twenty-one years old. Its programs were operated by private corporations, state or federal agencies, universities, and other nonprofit institutions. On-the-job training in private industry and supportive services for hard-core unemployed or underemployed persons between eighteen and twenty-two were funded under the JOBS program. And both classroom instruction and on-the-job training were offered for recipients of aid to families with dependent children (AFDC) under the WIN program. To provide incentives for WIN recipients, their AFDC allowances were reduced by only 67 percent of each dollar they earned over $30 per month, while nonparticipants' allowances were reduced by 100 percent.

In the early seventies, these and other manpower programs came under attack. Yet serious evaluations of the effectiveness of the programs indicate that some have represented a far more productive use of public funds than the alternatives they replaced. In seven studies of MDTA programs, for instance, all but one found very high rates of return on the training expenditures for individual programs; the rates ranged from 12.2 percent

2. *Manpower Report of the President—April 1974*, p. 358.
3. Ibid.

to 138.0 percent per annum.[4] The one exception estimated that the return for on-the-job training was large (49 percent) but that the return on institutional training was small (6.3 percent).[5] All of the studies concluded that on-the-job training had a higher rate of return than institutional training: institutional training costs tend to be about $2,000 per trainee, while on-the-job training costs ranged around $485;[6] yet the benefits they render in terms of increased earnings potential are similar.

Other federal manpower programs appear not to have been very effective; they have not been studied as carefully as the MDTA programs, however. The primary goals of the Neighborhood Youth Corps were to prevent youths from dropping out of school and provide working and training opportunities for those who were dropouts. The focus was on jobs; the training component of the program was strengthened, however, after it was criticized. Analyses of the program's benefits as related to its costs have not been encouraging. Furthermore, one critique concludes that the program was not influential in reducing dropout rates or in raising the educational aspirations and achievements of enrollees.[7]

Preliminary studies of the Job Corps program are also unencouraging. The most optimistic estimates of the program's impact fail to project much value received for the investments made.[8] The WIN and JOBS programs have been criticized for their lack of effectiveness and poor administration, although no really reliable quantitative studies of them have been done.[9] Training is only a secondary goal of WIN, of course; its purpose is to encourage welfare recipients to work. The financial incentives it offers are not great, however, and the program's administration is en-

4. Jon H. Goldstein, *The Effectiveness of Manpower Training Programs: A Review of Research on the Impact on the Poor,* staff study prepared for the Subcommittee on Fiscal Policy of the Joint Economic Committee of Congress (GPO, 1972), p. 29.

5. David O. Sewell, *Training the Poor, A Benefit-Cost Analysis of Manpower Programs in the U.S. Antipoverty Program* (Kingston, Ontario: Industrial Relations Centre, Queens University, 1971), pp. 78–81; cited in Goldstein, *The Effectiveness of Manpower Training Programs,* p. 29.

6. Garth L. Mangum, *MDTA: Foundation of Federal Manpower Policy* (Johns Hopkins University Press, 1968), p. 121.

7. Gerald D. Robin, *An Assessment of the In-Public School Neighborhood Youth Corps Projects in Cincinnati and Detroit with Special Reference to Summer-Only and Year-Round Enrollees* (Philadelphia: National Analysts, Inc., 1969), p. iii.

8. Goldstein, *The Effectiveness of Manpower Training Programs,* p. 48.

9. See ibid., pp. 6–11 and 50–61.

cumbered by the demand that administrators spend time enforcing restrictions and penalties imposed on noncooperating welfare recipients.

From the evaluations of federal manpower programs it appears that only the MDTA, which clearly focuses on training and manpower development, has been reasonably successful in achieving its goals.

To remedy some of the deficiencies in manpower programs, the numerous programs authorized under the MDTA and title one of the Economic Opportunity Act were loosely combined under the Comprehensive Employment and Training Act of 1973. It was hoped that if the programs were decentralized and decategorized, they might be able to provide services more specific to the needs of individual communities. The bulk of the authorizations under the 1973 act goes for comprehensive manpower services (specified in title one), which include institutional and on-the-job training, counseling and placement services, retraining allowances, and other financial and personal services designed to smooth the transition between jobs. The programs are, for the most part, administered by prime sponsors, which may be states, governments of localities whose population exceeds 100,000, or combinations of local governments. Most of these funds are apportioned among the states on the basis of a weighted average of each state's manpower allotment, level of unemployment, and number of adults in low-income families in the previous year.

Of the $3.7 billion that Congress authorized for manpower programs for fiscal 1975, more than 40 percent was designated for comprehensive manpower assistance. More than a third of the funds was allocated to public service employment programs (specified in titles two and six of the 1973 act), and a quarter was allocated to nationwide programs, such as the Job Corps, as well as special programs for the disadvantaged as determined by the secretary of labor. The aim of giving local officials more flexibility in designing programs has been fulfilled only in part.[10]

An important adjunct to federal manpower training programs is the federal-state employment service system, administered through fifty-four separate state employment services with over two thousand local offices. The main function of the services is to refer qualified workers to employers with job openings.

10. William Mirengoff and Lester Rindler, *The Comprehensive Employment and Training Act: Impact on People Places Programs, An Interim Report* (National Academy of Sciences, 1976), p. 24.

With the passage of the Manpower Development and Training Act of 1962 and the Economic Opportunity Act of 1964, the U.S. Employment Service assumed the additional responsibilities of counseling individuals seeking work and placing them in MDTA, Neighborhood Youth Corps, and Job Corps training programs. The Economic Opportunity Act also created neighborhood-centered community action agencies to locate the out-of-work poor and place them in paying jobs. The community action agencies thus became competitors of the U.S. Employment Service and thereby stimulated the employment services to increased activism.[11]

Strong federal manpower programs that can match supply and demand for job skills are seen by some advocates as a major component of a strategy to reduce unemployment. One study argues that an expansion of manpower programs combined with improvements in the federal-state employment service system, youth counseling, child-care support, and payments of relocation allowances could reduce the unemployment rate by more than 2 percentage points while entailing an incremental cost of about $14 billion per year.[12] Such an approach, if successful, would substantially help workers adversely affected by foreign trade and would probably alleviate the need to provide special programs for them alone. Of course, the success of this strategy depends on the validity of the assumption that U.S. unemployment is a structural problem. Critics of this approach argue that training merely rearranges the order in which individuals are hired.

Income Maintenance Programs

Income maintenance programs that provide financial support for workers during periods of unemployment or adverse circumstances such as disability can greatly cushion the adverse effects of economic dislocation. Some types of income maintenance programs, both government and private, can help to ease the dislocations caused by import competition.

11. U.S. President's Commission on Income Maintenance Programs, *Poverty Amid Plenty: The American Paradox* (GPO, 1969), p. 100.

12. Charles C. Holt and others, *Manpower Programs to Reduce Inflation and Unemployment: Manpower Lyrics for Macro Music* (Washington: Urban Institute, December 1971), pp. III-2 and III-3.

Unemployment Insurance

The program of greatest importance to unemployed workers is the system of unemployment insurance. All of the states now have their own unemployment insurance programs and they administer special unemployment insurance programs for federal employees and military veterans. The Federal Railroad Retirement Board administers a program for railroad employees.

Workers become eligible for benefits under unemployment insurance after a specified period of employment. An eligible worker must neither leave his job voluntarily nor be dismissed for misconduct. He must be able and available to take a job and must accept suitable work if it is offered to him.[13] The length of time for which benefits may be paid depends on the applicant's work history and previous unemployment insurance benefits received.

Unemployment benefits are fairly low relative to the wages workers receive while employed and they vary considerably from state to state. The maximum weekly benefits, including allowances for dependents, in May 1975 varied from $156 in Connecticut to $60 in Mississippi.[14] The actual levels of benefits, on the other hand, averaged $68.75 in the entire United States in February 1975, ranging from $89.66 in the District of Columbia to $48.47 in Mississippi.[15] Weekly benefits in 1939 had averaged about 50 percent of the covered wage in every state. By 1968, they averaged only 34 percent for the nation as a whole but varied between 31 percent and 60 percent by state.[16] After 1968, average benefits as a percentage of covered wage levels improved somewhat, reaching 38 percent in February 1975.[17]

13. For a discussion of the work requirement and problems in its administration see Raymond Munts, "Work Tests: A Review of Issues," in Larry L. Orr, Robinson G. Hollister, and Myron J. Lefcowitz, eds., *Income Maintenance: Interdisciplinary Approaches to Research* (Markham, 1971), pp. 239–57.

14. Senate Finance Committee, *Staff Data and Materials on Unemployment Compensation* (GPO, 1975), pp. 16–18.

15. U.S. Department of Labor, Manpower Administration, *Unemployment Insurance Statistics* (April 1975).

16. President's Commission on Income Maintenance Programs, *Poverty Amid Plenty*, p. 109.

17. The average covered wage figure is hard to come by. In 1974 the average private nonagricultural wage was $154.45 per week (*Manpower Report of the President—April 1975*, p. 282), and by February 1975 it had grown to $157.44 (BLS, *Employment and Earnings*, May 1975, table C-2). The average covered

Between 1968 and 1974, unemployment insurance coverage was extended to several new classes of employees, including employees of small firms and most employees of state governments and nonprofit institutions. In June 1974 more than 70 million workers were covered, accounting for about 89.4 percent of total nonagricultural employment in the United States,[18] as compared to 80 percent in 1968.[19]

Unemployment insurance is financed by a federal payroll tax. Employers may claim a partial credit on this payroll tax if it is paid to a federally approved state unemployment insurance plan. Federal law requires states to base the taxes of individual employers on experience ratings, so that employers that lay off or fire workers often are required to make larger than average contributions.

The availability of unemployment insurance benefits is an important factor in determining whether a trade adjustment assistance program for workers is necessary or useful. Much of the benefit to workers from trade adjustment assistance amounts to an increase in unemployment insurance benefits. In fact, the Nixon administration, in introducing its trade reform bill to Congress in 1973, chose to play down adjustment assistance and promised instead to submit legislation to reform and improve the level of unemployment insurance benefits. In a bill introduced by Congressman William Steiger of Wisconsin, the administration proposed to reduce the variation in state benefit levels and to increase the average somewhat by setting a federally imposed floor on benefits equal to 50 percent of the average weekly wage of covered workers.

As the administration's trade bill became transformed by Congress into the Trade Act of 1974, its adjustment assistance provisions were greatly strengthened and the Steiger bill became less relevant for trade-impacted workers.

Welfare Programs

Several types of welfare programs provide income supplements during periods of unemployment. The AFDC-UF program (aid to families with

---

weekly wage for 1974 was $175.57 (data provided by BLS); the figure for February 1975 was estimated by assuming the same growth rate for both the covered wage and the private nonagricultural wage.

18. BLS, *Employment and Wages,* 2nd quarter, 1974, table A-1.

19. President's Commission on Income Maintenance Programs, *Poverty Amid Plenty,* p. 109.

dependent children—unemployed father) is an extension of the standard AFDC program, which is funded by the federal government as well as by states and localities. It is administered by the states under widely varying eligibility and benefit level rules.[20] It really is of little relevance to the average displaced worker, especially one who had been earning a fairly high wage. Many states include among their eligibility criteria limitations on family resources that may require some households to liquidate asset holdings. Also, some states consider the income of relatives when measuring a household's income against the AFDC standard, and some demand a lien on the household's property before they will administer AFDC. Most important, the benefits are not particularly high—the average AFDC-UF family in July 1974 received monthly benefits of $297,[21] which was roughly comparable to unemployment insurance benefits. The AFDC-UF payments also suffer by comparison with unemployment benefits available to the highly paid worker, since AFDC benefit levels are not tied to the displaced worker's former earnings. It would appear that AFDC-UF is most useful to the worker who is no longer eligible for unemployment insurance.

One program under which families with relatively high incomes may receive a subsidy is the food stamp program. The amount of subsidy varies with income level; for example, the January–June 1975 schedule allowed a family of five with a net income as high as $606 per month to purchase $182 worth of food stamps per month for $154, for a subsidy of $336 per year. But if the family had earned less than $30 per month, it would have paid nothing for the $182 worth of food stamps, and its annual subsidy would have been $2,184.[22]

Supplemental Unemployment Benefits and Wage Guarantees

In addition to government programs of income maintenance, displaced workers may be protected by guarantees available under collective bargaining agreements. Income security became an important issue in collec-

20. *Handbook of Public Income Transfer Programs: 1975*, staff study prepared for the Subcommittee on Fiscal Policy of the Joint Economic Committee of Congress (GPO, 1974), p. 145.

21. Ibid., p. 167.

22. For a definition of net income, as well as an outline of eligibility requirements, application procedures, and benefit levels, see Kathryn Michelman and Joe Richardson, "How the Food Stamp Program Works: A Resource Paper" (Congressional Research Service, Jan. 7, 1975; processed).

tive bargaining in the early fifties. In 1955 a supplemental unemployment benefit (SUB) plan was negotiated for employees of the Ford Motor Company belonging to the United Automobile, Aerospace and Agricultural Implement Workers of America (UAW). Other companies in the automobile and farm equipment industries quickly followed suit and were joined by firms in the primary and fabricated metals, rubber, flat glass, women's apparel, cement, and maritime industries. The coverage of SUB plans has increased very little since 1956 because workers added through new agreements have been offset by declines in employment in the major SUB industries.[23] In 1963 about 1.9 million workers had SUB coverage, or about 25 percent of the 7.5 million workers included in a survey of major collective bargaining agreements.[24] A study ten years later of about 6.7 million workers covered by 1,339 collective bargaining agreements revealed that 218 contracts had SUB plans, protecting 1.9 million workers, or about a third of the sample.[25]

Most SUB plans are designed to provide weekly supplements to state unemployment insurance benefits. They often provide benefits for partially employed as well as unemployed workers. In 1963 the total weekly benefit payment for fully unemployed workers in SUB plans, including state unemployment insurance benefits, other earnings, and SUB, ranged from 55 percent to 80 percent of weekly wages. Most steelworkers' plans called for 60 percent and most automobile workers and all rubberworkers' plans specified 62 percent. Most plans also paid a supplement of $1.50 to $2.00 a week for each dependent.[26]

Under most SUB plans the period of eligibility for benefit payments is determined by time credits accumulated while working. Usually, a worker can accumulate a maximum of fifty-two weeks of eligibility, though some plans limit the maximum eligibility to twenty-six or thirty-nine weeks.[27]

The Ford-UAW plan and other SUB plans patterned after it also pro-

23. BLS, *Major Collective Bargaining Agreements: Supplemental Unemployment Benefit Plans and Wage-Employment Guarantees,* bulletin 1425-3 (GPO, 1965), p. 1.

24. Ibid., pp. 4 and 78.

25. BLS, *Characteristics of Agreements Covering 1,000 Workers or More: July 1, 1973,* bulletin 1822 (GPO, 1974), p. 62.

26. BLS, *Supplemental Unemployment Benefit Plans and Wage-Employment Guarantees,* p. 9.

27. Ibid., p. 86.

vided for health insurance premiums for the laid-off workers and their dependents. A maximum of twelve months' premiums was reimbursable.[28]

Collective bargaining arrangements have also included wage-employment guarantees that insure workers of either pay or employment for the duration of the guarantee period, which varies from one week to a year. A Labor Department study revealed that of the 7.5 million workers covered under major collective bargaining agreements in 1963, 602,000 had work-employment guarantees. Five out of six of those workers were covered by weekly guarantees and only six agreements, covering 12,500 workers, contained a guaranteed annual wage.[29] However, the portion of workers covered had risen from 8 percent in the 1963 sample to about 14.5 percent of all workers in a 1973 survey.[30]

Despite the existence of various types of income maintenance plans, the typical worker displaced by import competition, technological change, or government policy decisions must substantially reduce his consumption or begin to liquidate his assets. The financial squeeze becomes greater as time passes without new employment. The typical middle-aged worker in 1974 would have been eligible for a maximum of twenty-six to thirty-six weeks of unemployment insurance benefits, depending on his home state, a possible total of fifty-two weeks with supplemental unemployment benefits. He might also have been immediately eligible for subsidized food stamp purchases (neither unemployment insurance payments nor food stamps are subject to tax). However, if a worker loses his job in an industry subject to frequent layoffs, he may have accumulated credits for less than the maximum eligibility under both unemployment insurance and SUB plans. Furthermore, if the plant at which he worked is permanently shut down or his firm or subsidiary is liquidated, his SUB benefits will be limited by the amount of money available in the SUB fund. For example, when the Studebaker plant in South Bend closed, the fund was nearly exhausted, so workers got virtually no SUB benefits (see chapter 6).

Although unemployment and SUB benefits may be exhausted, the worker may be eligible for welfare in the form of medicaid or AFDC-UF. Income from these sources, however, is likely to be far below unemployment benefits. Furthermore, even a much more generous and broad in-

28. Ibid., p. 31.
29. Ibid., p. 88.
30. BLS, *Characteristics of Agreements,* p. 62.

come maintenance plan would leave the average worker's level of income far below what he had earned or might earn if he were able to find similar new employment.

Additional Security through Collective Bargaining

Supplemental unemployment benefits and wage-employment guarantees, which provide some protection to the worker who is displaced or would be displaced in the absence of guarantees, are the result of private collective bargaining agreements. There is a wide range of other kinds of provisions in collective bargaining arrangements that either protect a worker from job displacement or help ease the financial and psychological burdens in the period immediately before and after displacement. These include provisions such as advance notice of plant closing, of major employer decisions affecting jobs, or of termination of a worker's employment; separation pay, sometimes given in lieu of advance notice; early retirement, and vesting and portability of pension rights; differential payments for workers required to shift to lower paying jobs; job counseling, placement, and training services for displaced workers; rights to transfer either within or between plants; benefits to transferring employees, such as relocation allowances, maintenance of wages, training or retraining, seniority, portability of fringe benefits, and flow-back rights; attrition agreements; vesting and portability of rights to fringe benefits such as health insurance and life insurance; and funding rules for fringe benefit programs, including pensions and SUB plans, to insure payment of vested rights to benefits if the employer should become insolvent.

Advance Notice Provisions

There are few standards regarding advance notice provisions in labor contracts. Many contracts stipulate that "reasonable" advance notice be given to workers who are to be permanently laid off, but they include no such requirement for workers to be laid off temporarily with recall rights. Precise provisions for advance notice usually specify a very short period, typically one week. Often they are part of labor-management contracts dealing with plant closings or relocations. A 1969 study of 1,823 major collective bargaining agreements covering 7.3 million workers found that almost 1 million were covered by contract provisions regarding advance notice or labor participation in decisions to close or relocate plants.[31] In a 1973 survey such provisions covered more than 1 million workers in a sample that was more than 600,000 workers smaller than the one for the 1969 study.[32] The required advance notice of plant closing varied considerably, ranging from one week to six months. In the meat packing industry, periods of advance notice were typically ninety days. Some contracts did not provide for specific notice of plant closings but required labor consultation and participation in management decisions to relocate plants; in effect this provides a warning at least that management is seriously considering closing facilities. Some contracts provide both advance notice of a plant closing and a separate notice to each individual employee regarding his termination date.[33]

Advance notice may also be required when a firm decides to install new equipment. For example, a labor contract of the Chicago Newspaper Publishers' Association requires that four months' advance notice be given before the installation of computerized typesetting equipment.[34] A contract between the Wyandotte Worsted Company and the Textile Workers Union of America specified that the union meet to discuss any proposed installation of new machinery at least two weeks before a change is made.[35] In fact, of the employees sampled in a 1973 study, 18.6 percent worked under contracts requiring some sort of advance notice of technological change.[36]

Advance notice of plant closing or termination of employment can cause problems for employers. If workers leave in large numbers before they are terminated, the operation of the plant may be disrupted. Employers, however, often have options that can prevent this from occurring. For example, contracts quite often release the employer from liability to give severance pay to workers who quit voluntarily.[37] A worker would

31. BLS, *Major Collective Bargaining Agreements: Plant Movement, Transfer, and Relocation Allowances,* bulletin 1425-10 (GPO, 1969), pp. 4–6.

32. BLS, *Characteristics of Agreements,* p. 61.

33. See BLS, *Plant Movement, Transfer, and Relocation Allowances,* pp. 6–10.

34. Herbert J. Blitz, ed., *Labor-Management Contracts and Technological Change: Case Studies and Contract Clauses* (Praeger, 1969), p. 13.

35. Ibid., p. 255.

36. BLS, *Characteristics of Agreements,* p. 61.

37. For a description of general eligibility requirements for severance pay under various contracts, see BLS, *Major Collective Bargaining Agreements: Severance Pay and Layoff Benefit Plans,* bulletin 1425-2 (GPO, 1965), pp. 15–23.

have little incentive to quit prematurely if his loss of severance pay exceeded any increase in pay that he could obtain by quitting to assume a new job. Other vested rights to fringe benefits, such as pensions and continued access to group health and life insurance, might also be jeopardized.

In many countries, requirements for advance notice are specified in legislation governing labor contracts or in other laws and regulations. For example, in Canada, 1972 legislation required all employers of more than fifty workers to provide advance notice. The advance notice required varies from eight to sixteen weeks depending on the size of the employer. In the United Kingdom the Contracts of Employment Act of 1963 as amended in 1972 requires one to eight weeks' notice depending on the employee's length of service. In Sweden, an agreement between the government Labor Market Board and the Swedish Employment Association requires two months' advance notice of termination of employment or plant closings.[38]

Severance Pay

Severance pay may in some cases be given in lieu of advance notice, although most separation pay agreements are not tied to any advance notice provisions. A 1963 survey of 1,773 collective bargaining agreements covering 7.5 million workers revealed that severance pay plans appeared in 525 plans involving 3.1 million workers.[39] Such provisions seem to have become more prevalent during the 1960s. For example, in 1963 six of eighteen contracts studied in the petroleum refining industry called for severance pay, compared to only two of twenty-seven in 1955.[40] Since 1963 the popularity of severance pay seems to have risen—in 1973 the contracts of 3.1 million workers, in a sample of 6.7 million, had such provisions.[41]

The amount of pay varied considerably and almost always depended on a worker's length of service. By 1963, agreements that specified benefits in additional weeks of pay provided an average of 11.0 weeks' severance pay for workers with ten years of service and 31.8 weeks of payments

38. General Agreement on Tariffs and Trade, COM. TD/W/92/Add. 3, April 21, 1969, p. 8.

39. BLS, *Severance Pay and Layoff Benefit Plans*, pp. 15–23.

40. BLS, *Technological Trends in Major American Industries*, bulletin 1474 (GPO, 1966), p. 183.

41. BLS, *Characteristics of Agreements*, p. 62.

after twenty-five years of service.[42] The maximum for workers with over twenty-five years of service varied from 7 weeks to 105 weeks.[43] Many plans specified payments in terms of a percentage of accumulated pay or in fixed dollar amounts that varied with the number of years of service.

Most severance pay plans were not specially funded, although there had been a significant growth in funded arrangements, particularly among large companies in the rubber, automobile, and farm machinery industries. In 1963, funded plans applied to 42 percent of the workers protected by severance benefits.[44] Many SUB plans also contained severance pay arrangements for permanently laid-off workers, for which funding was tied to the financing of SUB benefits.

In some states, severance pay provisions can either disqualify a worker or reduce his period of eligibility for unemployment insurance benefits. For example, in 1971 receipt of wages in lieu of notice was grounds for disqualification from unemployment insurance benefits in eleven states, while dismissal payments disqualified workers in six states. Provision for wages in lieu of benefits led to prorated reductions in unemployment benefits in twenty-two states, and dismissal payments caused benefit reductions in thirteen.[45] State laws are not always clear on this matter, so that often decisions concerning benefit levels are based on administrative, not statutory, criteria, which can vary depending on the person making the decisions. The discrepancies in treatment among states could be removed if standards were specified in federal unemployment insurance legislation. As in the case of advance notice, some other countries have national standards regarding severance pay, like the U.K. redundancy payments scheme discussed in chapter 9.

Early Retirement

The retirement age that most pension plans specify is sixty-five, although there has been a trend toward lowering the age. Many plans now permit normal retirement at sixty, and others enable employees to retire

42. BLS, *Severance Pay and Layoff Benefit Plans,* p. 44. The figures show a slight increase in benefits over those of a 1955–56 study, in terms of average weeks of pay.

43. Ibid., p. 50.

44. Ibid., p. 11.

45. Department of Labor, Manpower Administration, *Comparison of State Unemployment Insurance Laws* (1972), pp. 4–55.

even before the normal retirement age. The Bureau of Labor Statistics found that plans covering 92 percent of the employees in a 1971 survey contained early retirement options.[46] This represents a substantial increase over the approximately 65 percent of workers in a 1959 survey who had a right to early retirement benefits.[47] Much of this increase occurred under multiemployer contracts: while only 13 percent of workers were eligible for early retirement under such contracts in 1959, 79 percent were eligible in 1971.[48]

Early retirement usually means the worker receives substantially lower annual payments than at normal retirement age. This may be due to the longer period over which payments can be expected to be made or to the worker's having accumulated fewer retirement credits. Only 5 percent of the workers under contracts in the 1971 survey with early retirement provisions could retire early at full benefits.[49]

About one in six retirement plans, however, allows for special early retirements.[50] These special retirements apply to workers who are severed involuntarily—when plant shutdowns occur or when management weeds out workers whose productivity or skills are low. Special early retirement plans are found in the automobile, rubber, and steel industries and offer substantially higher benefits than those granted under most contracts.[51]

Both regular and special early retirement plans usually require a displaced worker both to be above a certain age and to have long service, at least part of which must be continuous. Many older workers are hence left uncovered by either early or normal retirement provisions. For example, a worker who held employment in a number of different firms for forty or fifty years may never have worked in one of them long enough to acquire the rights to a pension. Even a worker who stayed with one firm for many years may lose pension rights because of breaks in service during extended layoffs or periods of disability, or because he transferred or was promoted within his firm or its subsidiaries to plants or departments

46. BLS, *Early Retirement Provisions of Pension Plans, 1971,* report 429 (1974), p. 3.

47. BLS, *Pension Plans Under Collective Bargaining,* bulletin 1284 (GPO, 1961), p. 40.

48. Ibid., p. 40, and BLS, *Early Retirement Provisions,* p. 3.

49. Ibid.

50. Ibid.

51. Merton C. Bernstein, *The Future of Private Pensions* (London: Free Press of Glencoe, 1964), p. 23.

with different pension plan requirements. Rules regarding pension rights are often so complicated that the worker is ill-informed and has little ability to protect his rights.[52]

Pension Vesting, Funding, and Portability

Congress in 1974 enacted legislation governing the control of pension funds and the individual's right to funds set aside in his name. Under the Employee Retirement Income Security Act of 1974 (ERISA) an individual is entitled to at least a percentage of his full pension rights after a specified period of service.[53] Though many pension plans had included vesting in one form or another, the provisions were so varied and there were so many inequities that federal standards became necessary. All private plans must now include at the minimum either full vesting after ten years of service, but none until the tenth year; 25 percent vesting after five years of service, with a gradual increase to 100 percent after fifteen years; or 50 percent vesting when the sum of the employee's age and his years of service reaches forty-five, with a gradual increase to 100 percent over the following five years.

At the time of the passage of the ERISA, according to some estimates, one-third of all the pension plans in force were insufficiently funded, and some corporations and unions were as much as forty years behind in their fund contributions.[54] The ERISA requires that the management of pension funds be placed in the hands of a qualified agency, such as an insurance company, which must invest prudently. Furthermore, the act specifies fines for noncontributors and establishes a Pension Benefit Guaranty Corporation, similar to the Federal Desposit Insurance Corporation, within the Department of Labor to insure pension payments.

While the legislation provides needed reforms of pension plans, far more needs to be done. The funding provisions are weak and it will take a long time to provide substantial security for workers in firms or industries with a low chance of survival. The only sure protection to workers is 100 percent funding of pension benefits. The ERISA also fails to provide

52. For a discussion of these problems see Ralph Nader and Kate Blackwell, *You and Your Pension* (Grossman, 1973). Some of these inequities are remedied by the Employment Retirement Income Security Act of 1974.

53. 88 Stat. 829-1035.

54. *New York Times,* Sept. 3, 1974.

for pension portability, under which a worker could obtain vested pension rights on the basis of accumulated work experience with several different firms. There are some multiemployer plans that provide portability, but the employers subscribing to these plans are mostly small firms.[55]

Plant Transfers and Relocation

Large firms with a number of plants or subsidiaries may provide assistance to displaced workers through interplant transfers. Under some labor contracts, when a single plant is shut down, when a plant moves from one location to another, or when the work force is reduced, workers are provided with protection and transfer rights either to a new plant or to other existing plants. Transfer provisions have become an integral part of agreements in nearly every industry except construction. In some industries such as steel, meat packing, and automobiles, there are extensive and detailed rules governing worker transfers. In a 1973 BLS study of 1,339 contracts, 485, covering 54 percent of the workers in the sample, contained provisions for interplant transfer or preferential hiring.[56]

When workers are transferred because their plant moves from one location to another, problems are often not as acute as they are when a plant closes down; when workers are transferred to existing plants, the rights of the workers already in those plants must also be protected. Frequently, different locals of the same union or different unions must bargain among themselves over seniority status and bumping rights of incoming workers. Rights to transfer to other plants vary among labor agreements. In some cases, displaced workers have nothing more than preferential hiring rights. This kind of arrangement is not likely to affect the security of, or to generate opposition from, employees at the receiving plant unless workers with preferential hiring rights are also given substantial seniority. Another relatively peaceful arrangement is the transfer of a whole department from one plant to another. Frequently, transfers are made through a bidding system: when a job vacancy occurs in a particular plant, workers from other plants may bid for the job along with

55. For example, some glass container manufacturers have such a plan. See Blitz, *Labor-Management Contracts,* p. 5.

56. BLS, *Characteristics of Agreements,* p. 58. For a detailed study of transfer provisions, see BLS, *Plant Movement, Transfer, and Relocation Allowances.*

resident workers. The vacancy is filled on the basis of seniority and qualifications without regard for the plant location of the bidders for the job. A much rarer practice is the exercise of bumping rights between plants. Bumping, an established practice in most companies, is the right of a senior worker to take the job of another worker who has less seniority or fewer qualifications. It is exercised routinely within plants but seldom between plants.

The exercise of transfer rights is often limited by the worker's length of service or by specified circumstances, such as a plant shutdown. Transferees under some labor contracts, in specific circumstances, are granted full seniority; in others, the amount of seniority varies according to the reason for the transfer. Alternatively, workers may be granted full seniority with regard to eligibility for fringe benefits but limited seniority with respect to bumping rights in the new plant, and in some situations the transferred worker is treated as a new employee.[57]

An important provision in some contracts is flow-back rights granted to transferees. If by choice or of necessity a worker's service in the plant to which he has transferred is terminated, he may be granted the right to return to his old plant if it has not ceased operating, or the right to severance pay and early retirement if the plant has shut down or there are no vacancies available there. Various rules govern the rights of the returnee regarding seniority, job access, and fringe benefits.[58]

Many labor contracts dealing with transfers provide for workers' rights to training for job openings at other plants, maintenance of income at a level achieved in the former plant, and portability of fringe benefits. A transferred worker is often eligible for relocation allowances, and in some instances may receive help in selling his home. He may also be entitled to financial relief if he loses equity in the sale of a home or pays penalties for termination of a home leasing agreement.

The provisions regarding plant transfers vary from employer to employer, and it is difficult to know how much protection they provide to the displaced worker. However, as with pensions, a good case can be made that federal standards ought to be applied. A plant closing or relocation places burdens on local, state, and federal social service functions, and it generates political opposition to government policies that foster innova-

57. BLS, *Plant Movement, Transfer, and Relocation Allowances,* p. 75.
58. See ibid., pp. 50–54 and 76.

tion and change. Part of these costs, at least, ought to be borne by the firm that stands to benefit from closing inefficient operations or moving production to a more advantageous location.

Other Forms of Protection

A variety of other arrangements concerning assistance to displaced workers does not come under plant transfer provisions. For example, a worker whose job is downgraded may be guaranteed his previous wage, at least for a limited period of time. Provisions such as these may be found in the synthetic materials, plastic products, and footwear industries. Displaced workers may also be given job counseling and training for employment by other firms. Fringe benefits such as health and life insurance may be maintained for a time after layoff if the worker is willing to contribute. In some cases, extensions of fringe benefits are tied in with SUB plans (as in the automobile industry) while in others (such as the steel, airline, and meat packing industries), the maintenance of fringe benefits is separately negotiated.[59]

Some agreements limit the rights of management to relocate production or engage in massive layoffs. In the apparel industry in particular, contract provisions place limitations on plant movement. In other industries, agreements require reductions in the work force to be accomplished largely through natural attrition.

Conclusions

Very general income-maintenance programs based on welfare provide relatively little help to displaced workers other than those on the low end of the income scale. Many such welfare programs are designed to assist families that often have little income-earning potential anyway.

Employment-related programs such as unemployment insurance, supplemental unemployment benefits, and retraining programs offer more hope to the worker who desires an equivalent or better job and in the meantime wishes to maintain a reasonable income. These programs, however, need to be strengthened. Unemployment insurance provides relatively low benefits compared to the previous earnings of many workers,

59. Blitz, *Labor-Management Contracts,* pp. 5–7.

and benefits vary considerably from state to state. Supplemental unemployment benefit programs are not widespread. Though the rationale for the Manpower Development and Training Act was basically to provide retraining to workers so as to combat structural unemployment, later programs have sought to attack a wide variety of social problems of the displaced worker.

Perhaps the best provisions for worker security and for easing the transition from one job to another are those found in collective bargaining agreements. Advance notice of termination enables a worker to search for a new job while his old one is in jeopardy. Job counseling, placement and training services, and interplant transfer rights help smooth job changes. Severance pay, early retirement, and improvements in vesting, funding, and portability of pensions provide income security when a worker, especially an older one who will have trouble finding new employment, loses his job. Yet there are almost no federally imposed standards regarding these matters. Instead, they are contained in collective bargaining agreements that vary a great deal.

CHAPTER EIGHT

Industry Approaches to Adjustment

INTERNATIONAL TRADE is not the only cause of economic change that evokes fears of unemployment. In the early sixties there was considerable talk about the job implications of increased automation. Recently, opposition to the movement to improve the environment has focused on the unemployment and waste of resources that might result from strict enforcement of environmental controls. The ways in which technological change was handled in two industries—the railroad and meat packing industries—are examined in this chapter. In the former industry, emphasis was placed on compensation, while in the latter a program was instituted that emphasized retraining and relocation.

The Railroad Industry

Employment on the railroads has had a long history of stagnation and decline. The number of workers in the industry in 1939 was only about one-third higher than in 1890 despite the fact that between those dates railroad output almost quadrupled.[1] Employment declined only slightly immediately after World War II, but began to drop sharply around 1950.

1. Harold Barger, *The Transportation Industries 1889–1946: A Study of Output, Employment, and Productivity* (National Bureau of Economic Research, 1951), pp. 96–97.

Between 1951 and 1961, employment on major railroad lines dropped by almost 44 percent, from 1.3 million to 0.7 million. From 1951 to 1973, railroad employment declined at a rate of about 2.8 percent per year.[2]

The poor employment picture in the railroad industry is due as much to the decline in the railroads' competitive position in the field of transport as it is to the industry's substantial gains in worker productivity due to technological improvements, increased capital per worker, and managerial efficiencies. In 1943, railroads accounted for 71.3 percent of all intercity freight traffic.[3] By 1972 this ratio had declined to 33.5 percent, with increased shares of traffic going by truck, pipeline, water, and air.[4]

Loss of jobs has been an important concern of railway labor organizations for many years and labor leaders have tried to stem the loss through legislation. In 1928 the movement for a "six-hour day" was launched at the convention of the Brotherhood of Railroad Trainmen in a resolution that expressed concern over the alarming rate of mechanization of railway jobs and the resulting displacement of labor. Throughout the thirties appeals were made to the President and Congress to enact legislation establishing a six-hour day in the hope that this would spread the work and save jobs, but the railway labor executives were not successful in achieving their goal.

Railroad labor lobbyists were successful, however, in having a protective provision inserted in the Emergency Railroad Transportation Act, passed by Congress in 1933. The act, which established a federal coordinator of transportation, was intended to encourage consolidations of railroad services and to improve the financial viability of American railroad companies. But the labor protective provision essentially nullified any incentives for consolidation since the number of employees of any railroad could not be reduced, nor could any worker be put out of work or have his pay reduced as a result of any action taken under the statute. Only a few minor coordinations were effected under the act.

When the act expired in 1935, the railway labor leaders attempted to maintain their job protection guarantees by collective bargaining with the

2. U.S. Interstate Commerce Commission, *66th Annual Report* (Government Printing Office, 1952), p. 215, and *88th Annual Report* (GPO, 1974), p. 122; statistics on class I line-haul railroads.

3. James C. Nelson, *Railroad Transportation and Public Policy* (Brookings Institution, 1959), p. 10.

4. ICC, *88th Annual Report,* p. 121.

railroads. Negotiations culminated in the Washington Agreement of May 21, 1936, between nearly all the major railroads and the railway unions. Workers affected by a coordination or consolidation of services between two or more carriers were to receive displacement allowances equal to 60 percent of their average wage at the time of displacement; these allowances could continue for as long as five years for employees with fifteen or more years of service. Employees who were downgraded in their jobs could maintain their previous monthly wage rates. Also, workers could take a lump-sum payment in lieu of monthly allowances.

Again, in the Transportation Act of 1940, labor leaders were able to have protective arrangements made a condition in the Interstate Commerce Commission's approval of any consolidation, merger, or coordination between carriers. At a minimum, the carriers had to ensure that, for four years from the date of the consolidation, no employees would be placed in a worse position with respect to their employment, except for employees with less than four years' service, who were protected for a period equal to their length of service. The provisions of the Washington Agreement for reimbursing displaced employees were also made a part of the conditions the ICC set in approving consolidations.

In the late thirties, railway labor leaders had attempted to have the ICC demand labor protective provisions in petitions for abandonments as well as consolidations and mergers. The ICC refused the labor requests until a 1939 Supreme Court decision forced it to insert labor protective provisions in its approval of an abandonment.[5] In subsequent cases the ICC has been flexible in its requirement of labor protective provisions, taking into account the financial impact on carriers requesting abandonments. For example, an insolvent line seeking total abandonment may not be required to provide any job protection at all.

After World War II, labor's concern was focused on the problem of discontinuance of firemen on diesel locomotives. A relatively small number of diesel engines had been put into operation before the war, mainly as yard switchers, which did not use firemen. However, in the late thirties and after the war, labor was successful in having firemen installed on diesel engines in certain other types of service.

In 1956, in both the United States and Canada, the railroads notified the Brotherhood of Locomotive Firemen and Enginemen of their intention

5. *United States* v. *Lowden,* 308 U.S. 225 (1939).

to greatly reduce the number of firemen on diesel locomotives. The problem was particularly acute in Canada, where firemen were used on diesels in yard and freight service as well as passenger service. A Royal Commission report in 1957 recommended discontinuance of firemen in yard and freight service. In May 1958, an agreement was reached between the Canadian Pacific Railroad and the Brotherhood that included gradual elimination of firemen and a protective arrangement for workers who were about to be displaced. Workers with more than five years of service would have their jobs or compensation protected until retirement. Those with two to five years' service would be offered alternative employment as yardmen or trainmen or would be offered yardmen's or trainmen's wages until retirement. Men with less than two years of seniority were to be given only preference for employment with the Canadian Pacific Railroad. The railroad estimated the total cost of the provisions at $38 million but felt that it could eventually, after full dieselization of the yard and freight services, save $11.6 million per year.[6]

The firemen's dispute in the United States lasted much longer and was considerably more acrimonious. After a three-year moratorium on changes in work rules and wage demands, the railroad carriers in November 1959 served notice that they intended to change the work rules, giving themselves authority to decide whether or not to employ firemen. The unions of course opposed the proposed change, and to settle the issue President Eisenhower in November 1960 created the Presidential Railroad Commission. The commission concluded that firemen were not essential and recommended that the position be gradually abolished, through attrition of those with ten years of service or more and separation in accordance with the Washington Agreement of 1936 for others.[7] The unions again objected. After eighteen more months of haggling, Congress passed Public Law 88-108, creating an arbitration board to settle the dispute. The Award of Arbitration Board 282, which was to be in force for two years, allowed the carriers to eliminate firemen's jobs and permitted the union to veto up to 10 percent of the reductions. Essentially, firemen with ten years or more of seniority could keep their jobs, those with two to ten years would be protected until they were placed in another job, and those

6. Nelson, *Railroad Transportation and Public Policy,* p. 275.

7. U.S. Commission to Inquire Into a Controversy Between Certain Carriers and Certain of Their Employees, *Report of the Presidential Railroad Commission* (GPO, 1962), pp. 48–50.

with less than two years' seniority could be terminated in accordance with the Washington Agreement. The award, finally implemented on May 7, 1964, led to the eventual loss of an estimated 18,000 firemen's jobs.[8]

The award did not end the controversy, however. When its two-year term expired in March 1966, the carriers claimed that actions taken under the award were still in force, while the unions pressed for restoration of work rights and lost pay, a position that would have essentially nullified the award. The dispute dragged on in the courts and in the conference rooms until July 19, 1972, when an agreement was finally signed. The agreement's specifications on manning rules and separations were similar to those in the Award of Arbitration Board 282. However, the agreement stipulated that the position of fireman serve as an intermediate training step that all employees must go through before being promoted to the rank of locomotive engineer, and that all carriers must set up training programs for firemen.

The long dispute over maintenance of the fireman's position was a continuation of the battle over work rules that accompanied the decline of the railroad industry. When the federal government was finally forced to take control of a large part of the industry, it dealt so generously with displaced employees that the argument over perpetuation of the jobs those workers held ceased to be the central issue. The protective arrangements certified by Secretary of Labor J. D. Hodgson on April 16, 1971, in accordance with section 405c of the Rail Passenger Act of 1970, were the most generous in American railroad history. They applied to employees of twenty railroads included in the consolidation of rail passenger service under the government operation that eventually became known as Amtrak.

If an employee was discharged, he could receive a monthly dismissal allowance equal to his average monthly salary at the time of severance. If the worker took other employment, his monthly allotment was reduced by the amount of other compensation received. The allowance was to continue for six years, or for a shorter period equal to previous length of service. In addition, fringe benefits such as hospitalization, pensions, and life insurance were to be maintained over the same period. Any worker whose job was downgraded was guaranteed his previous monthly wage and fringe benefits, and his compensation was to be adjusted to reflect general wage increases for six years. The provisions offered protection to

8. Joseph F. Fulton, "The Railway Fireman Manning Dispute: History and Issues, 1959–1970" (U.S. Library of Congress, Legislative Reference Service, July 1970; processed), p. 20.

both union and nonunion members. Any employee whose job was terminated as a result of the consolidation was also granted priority over other applicants for a comparable position, even if he required retraining. Costs of retraining were paid by the railroad, as were moving, traveling, and living expenses of any employee who was retrained and required to change residence. The worker was reimbursed for any loss suffered in the sale of his home for less than fair value, or for the loss incurred through cancellation of a lease.

All costs of the protective provisions of the Amtrak agreement could be charged as a current expense during the first year of Amtrak's existence, even though actual payments for allowances and retraining would stretch over six years or more. The estimated cost of the provisions was about $80 million, of which $22 million was included in the Penn Central line's expenses.[9]

The Amtrak protective arrangements have often been cited as a precedent for trade adjustment assistance.[10] The protective provisions and severance pay arrangements in the railroad industry, which have been far more generous than such arrangements in other industries, reflect the considerable economic and political power of the railroad unions. They are the outgrowth of the unions' long involvement in railroad affairs, which the federal government has conspicuously aided through legislation and regulation. Governmental interest in protecting railroad workers is also evident in the federal government's sponsorship of the Railroad Retirement Fund and in the special unemployment compensation scheme for railroad workers.

The Meat Packing Industry

In sharp contrast to the railroad industry's compensation scheme for displaced workers, the meat packing industry attacked the employment problems brought on by modernization with programs to help workers

9. Economic and Finance Department, Association of American Railroads, Jan. 26, 1973. Five companies, including Penn Central, gave a detailed breakdown of the labor protection portion of their charges against the Amtrak agreement; the remaining fifteen companies are assumed to have assigned a like share of their Amtrak writeoff to labor protection.

10. See testimony of C. Fred Bergsten and Douglas A. Fraser in *Trade Adjustment Assistance,* hearings before the Subcommittee on Foreign Economic Policy of the House Committee on Foreign Affairs, 92:2 (GPO, 1972), pp. 125 and 326–29.

move into new jobs. The closing of outmoded plants in the four major packing houses in the 1950s had affected the jobs of 30,000 workers by 1961. When the impact of the upheaval on the employees of Armour and Company—the second largest in the industry—became evident, the company and the two unions that represented a majority of the affected workers began working on an assistance plan that improved each time it was put into use.

Between 1951 and 1959, Armour closed nine small plants in various parts of the country. Then, in 1959, it closed six large plants, including its main packing house in Chicago. The 1959 shutdowns eliminated 20 percent of the company's total capacity and terminated work for some 6,000 production employees. By 1965, six more plants that ranged in size from 180 to 1,600 employees had been closed. In total, as of mid-1965, Armour had shut down twenty-one plants and terminated employment of 14,000 workers in the course of a fifteen-year rationalization process.[11]

At the same time, Armour had built eight new plants which began operating in 1963 and 1964. These eight new units together employed only about 900 workers, reflecting the trend toward specialization and automation in the industry.[12]

For the most part, workers involved in the Armour layoffs had no skills that could be utilized in other jobs without additional training. The median age of the workers ranged from forty-five to forty-eight and the median level of education did not exceed the eighth grade. Many of the workers had begun working at Armour during the World War II and postwar labor shortage and had accumulated on the average some twenty years of seniority rights, so finding new employment was to be a new, uncomfortable, and difficult task for them. About 12–15 percent of the displaced workers were female and their average age exceeded that of the male workers. The composition of minority workers in the last six plants that were shut down varied considerably. In the Sioux City, Iowa, plant, only about 5 percent of the employees were either black or American Indian, whereas in the Kansas City plant 75 percent of the work force was black.[13]

Even in good circumstances, finding new jobs for the typical Armour worker would have been difficult, but the problem was magnified by slack

11. George P. Shultz and Arnold R. Weber, *Strategies for the Displaced Worker* (Harper and Row, 1966), p. 6. This book describes the Armour rationalization process, the subsequent labor negotiations, and the measures taken.

12. Ibid., p. 7.

13. Ibid., pp. 7–8.

labor markets. In all of the communities in which the last six plants were shut down, except for Sioux City, the local unemployment rate exceeded 5 percent or worsened considerably during the period that the employees were looking for work. In Sioux City, the relatively small labor market and the limited number of industrial jobs made finding new employment difficult.[14]

The problems of the displaced Armour workers were exacerbated by the fact that decisions to close the plants were made and put into effect quickly. Workers had little, if any, advance notice of the shutdowns and were rapidly separated from their jobs. This meant that the usual labor-reducing devices, such as attrition, early retirement, and bumping rights for workers with seniority, which might have cushioned the impact, were not well utilized.

Traditionally, Armour had been noted for progressive collective bargaining contracts. In its 1959 contract with the Amalgamated Meat Cutters and Butcher Workmen of North America, and the United Packinghouse, Food and Allied Workers, the company set up an automation fund committee made up of representatives from management, the unions, and the public. The duties of the committee included sponsoring research concerning the problems of displaced workers, promoting new employment opportunities within the company, providing training for displaced employees, giving allowances for moving expenses, and considering other programs and methods that might be used to assist displaced workers.[15]

The committee worked with a company-financed $500,000 fund. Initially it sponsored special research projects that set guidelines for later programs of retraining and worker loans. Among its early studies were surveys of workers' experience in finding new jobs after the Armour shutdowns. Not only had the workers found it difficult to get jobs as good as their former positions, but they were hard pressed to find any employment at all. Surveys taken two years after shutdowns in five cities showed that unemployment rates among these workers ranged from 25 percent to 53 percent and were especially high for olders workers, minority groups, the uneducated, and the unskilled.[16] Other early studies concentrated on policy questions such as advance notice of plant shutdowns, interplant transfers, and long-run prospects for employment in the meat packing industry.

In 1960, during the committee's fact-finding stage, a plant in Oklahoma

14. Ibid., p. 8.
15. Ibid., pp. 3–5.
16. Ibid., pp. 9–10.

City was shut down. The automation fund committee then put its first worker assistance program into action. The emphasis of this ad hoc attempt to aid the displaced workers was on placement and retraining. The placement efforts proved discouraging, for workers were most often referred to "the casual labor pool."[17] A survey of workers who did find jobs verified that most of them had done so on their own. The retraining efforts were hampered by the fact that the program got under way after the plant closed. Furthermore, for the most part, the workers with the most difficult rehiring problems—including blacks, women, and the uneducated—were admitted to the program. A study made in 1962 of those who were retrained showed that 46 percent were unemployed, as compared to 34 percent of the entire group of displaced workers. Of the twenty-two retrainees who were employed at the time, only six had found jobs that appeared to be related to their retraining.[18] The committee also introduced a plan to transfer workers to the Armour plant in Kansas City and to provide them with relocation allowances, but the plan was never implemented because of subsequent cutbacks in the number of workers in the Kansas City plant. Although the results in Oklahoma City were modest at best, the committee had begun to function.

The experience in Oklahoma City and the research projects that had been carried out led to a renegotiation of the collective bargaining agreement in 1961. Two clauses of the original contract were changed to increase severance payments and to improve pension benefits. Under the increased severance payment policy, workers who were subsequently laid off in Fort Worth, Texas, and Sioux City, Iowa, collected on the average a lump sum of approximately $3,000, thus imposing substantial direct costs on the company in these large-scale layoffs. The improved retirement benefits provided, in the event of a plant shutdown, early retirement benefits for employees who were at least fifty-five years old—as opposed to the previous cut-off age of sixty—and who had been with the company for twenty years.[19]

Three new concepts also were added to the 1961 contract. A minimum

17. Edwin Young, "The Armour Experience: A Case Study in Plant Shutdown," in Gerald G. Somers, Edward L. Cushman, and Nat Weinberg, eds., *Adjusting to Technological Change* (Harper and Row, 1963), p. 156.

18. Richard C. Wilcock and Walter H. Franke, *Unwanted Workers* (London: Free Press of Glencoe, 1963), p. 59.

19. Shultz and Weber, *Strategies for the Displaced Worker,* p. 11.

of ninety days' advance notice of a plant shutdown was to be given employees, during which all workers were guaranteed forty hours of employment each week. Any displaced worker under the age of sixty with at least one year of continuous service could exercise bumping rights at other Armour plants over any worker hired after the signing of the 1961 contract. Transferred workers were given seniority with regard to vacation pay and other fringe benefits but were treated as new workers in all other respects, including eligibility for severance pay and bumping rights in the new plant. During the period of transition, employees with five or more years of service could receive technological adjustment pay, which provided a minimum of $65 per week—the company paid the difference between unemployment compensation or other income received by the worker and $65. Relocation allowances were also given the workers up to a maximum of $520. Finally, the 1961 bargaining agreement provided for transferring displaced workers to eight new replacement plants that were to begin operating in 1963 and 1964. Displaced workers were given a preferred claim on these new jobs, but rather than detail a set of rules to be followed, the agreement specified that the automation fund committee should determine eligibility in each case.

With improvements in the 1961 agreement, the automation fund committee began to act more effectively in plant closings. The next shutdown, in Birmingham, Alabama, happened three months after the conclusion of negotiations. The plant employed only about 150 workers, who were easily placed in new jobs. Then, in the summer of 1962, the Fort Worth, Texas, plant, with a work force of 1,100, closed. The case was considered the first real test for the new provisions. The project to help the displaced workers began ninety days before the shutdown, as required. Employees were informed about transfers, placement, and retraining while still on the job. Plans called for the displaced employees to take advantage of the newly enacted Manpower Development and Training Act programs, but delays in implementation of the MDTA forced the committee to devise its own training programs.

Not many workers from Fort Worth used the interplant transfer program, since most of the job openings were in northern cities. Workers were reluctant to transfer so far away, especially since their loss of seniority meant reduced protection against subsequent layoffs. Furthermore, placement attempts in Fort Worth did not work much better than in Oklahoma City. Although the committee tried to convince community placement services that Armour employees should be given special attention, displaced workers were treated as routine placement cases. A random sampling of displaced workers who found jobs showed that only 3.5 percent attributed them to leads given by the employment services.[20]

The results of the retraining program in Fort Worth were somewhat more encouraging. Unlike Oklahoma City's, the program was designed so that retraining was available to everyone who wanted it. Again, however, no subsistence payments were made to retrainees from committee funds. Workers who did not receive substantial severance pay had to rely mainly on unemployment compensation and temporary and part-time employment as a source of income. Furthermore, under state law, persons engaged in full-time schooling were not "available for employment" and thus were ineligible for unemployment benefits, so most of the retrainees attended night school. Another problem was posed by the long duration of some of the training programs. In many instances trainees exhausted their unemployment benefit claims before completing their courses. Of the 170 people who started training in Fort Worth, 150 completed training, and 97.8 percent of those completing retraining and active in the labor market were employed within eighteen months of completion. Out of those, 58.5 percent held jobs that were directly or indirectly related to their training.[21]

The adjustment assistance program was most successful in the shutdown that took place next, in June 1963 in Sioux City, Iowa. Previous experience indicated that if the interplant transfer program was to be effective, it would have to be modified, so a new policy of providing flow-back rights was introduced. A transferring employee could return to his original home within three months without losing his claim to severance pay. This meant that the only potential money loss that could be envisioned by an employee whose transfer proved unsuccessful was the deduction from his severance pay of any technological adjustment payments and relocation allowances that the company had given him. Even though this provision was not written into the contract and was only experimental, in the subsequent shutdown in Kansas City, Missouri, flow-back rights were again exercised and displaced workers were far more willing to move. Interplant transfers were attractive to Sioux City workers because there were two

20. Ibid., p. 120.
21. Ibid., pp. 154, 157, and 163.

Armour plants relatively close by to which they could transfer. Of the total of 1,150 workers displaced in Sioux City, 234 did transfer. In the first seven months at their new jobs, 83 percent had had no more than ten days' interruption in employment due to layoffs.[22] Follow-up interviews indicated that most transferred workers were satisfied with their new jobs.

Placement efforts in Sioux City also proved more successful because of a modified approach. Three days after advance notice, the collection of data on all the workers began. Workers were given counseling and aptitude tests. By the time of the layoffs, the skills and potential of the workers had been widely publicized in the local labor market. The Iowa Employment Service gave special attention to the plant's displaced workers, and in the twenty-three months following the shutdown, 422 former Armour employees had been placed in jobs in the local labor market.[23]

Retraining in the Sioux City case was also considered successful. The committee was able to tap federal manpower programs, although Armour did set up supplemental programs. Relieved of the responsibility of administering all the training programs, the committee was able to concentrate on special problems that had stymied previous retraining programs. Two years after the plant shutdown, 156 employees had entered training programs—119 in federally supported centers and 37 in programs financed by Armour.[24] The costs of retraining were, for the first time, paid for by the federal government and Armour, respectively. And all trainees were given subsistence allowances. The federal manpower provisions stipulated that workers who were heads of households and were enrolled in an approved government training course could draw allowances equal to the average unemployment benefits in the state in the preceding quarter. They were eligible for this allowance for up to fifty-two weeks, and in Iowa the allowance averaged about $32 per week. Shortly after the Sioux City retraining programs began, amendments to the federal law provided supplementary allowances of $10 per week and workers were permitted to work up to twenty hours per week without forfeiting any of the training allowance. The Armour committee paid similar allowances for workers in their training programs. In addition to subsistence grants, the committee experimented with a loan program for workers undergoing training. Within

22. Ibid., pp. 58–60 and 69.
23. Ibid., p. 120.
24. Ibid., p. 137.

three to twelve months after completing their courses, 88.2 percent of the Sioux City trainees were employed, and 56 percent had found employment directly related to their training.[25]

In terms of numbers of people aided, the most successful case was the Kansas City plant, half of which was shut down in August 1964, and the other half in June 1965. Again the experience of the preceding incidents was instrumental to the committee's improved tactics.

Conclusions

The experiences in the railroad and meat packing industries are illustrative of two very different approaches to lessening the adverse economic impact of technological change in an industry. In the railroad industry, emphasis was placed on providing generous compensation for displaced workers. In the meat packing industry, the stress was on retraining and job transfers.

The generous protective arrangements for labor included in the Amtrak agreement are cited often by union officials as a good example of what can be done for workers. The railroad industry, however, is a very special case. The federal government has been involved in protecting railroad workers for a number of decades, and the very generous arrangements were partly the result of federal government enforcement and participation. It is not likely that such generous provisions would have emerged if they had been the result of purely private negotiations between the railroads and their workers. The labor protective arrangements were part of the price the railroads had to pay for federal financial and regulatory support. The railroads have long been criticized for adapting quite slowly to new work patterns required by a changing technology, but job protection arrangements have led to inefficient labor allocations in the railroad industry.

In the Armour meat packing case, emphasis was placed on helping workers adjust to new jobs rather than protecting them in their old jobs or paying lavish benefits for separated workers. Considered a responsive and forward looking company by union leaders, Armour was singled out as a proving ground for far-reaching innovations. The early plant shut-

25. Ibid., pp. 158 and 163.

downs in the protracted and planned rationalization of the industry set precedents for subsequent shutdowns. The establishment of a committee that used the feedback received in each incident to improve subsequent adjustments gave cohesion to the readjustment efforts. Armour was able to capitalize on federal manpower programs, as does the Defense Department's Office of Economic Adjustment. This suggests that a planned adjustment program can take advantage of existing programs and need not create a separate bureaucracy for every one of its functions.

CHAPTER NINE

Adjustment Assistance in Other Countries

THE TARGETS of adjustment assistance vary greatly from country to country. Canada is the only major industrial nation other than the United States whose programs are geared specifically toward workers and firms affected by increased imports. Most countries' assistance efforts have been designed without special regard to the factors causing industrial dislocation. The members of the European Community, however, have had assistance programs since the early fifties to help workers and firms affected by the integration of national markets.

Often, adjustment assistance programs in foreign countries are tailored to fit the needs of particular industries. Labor-intensive industries, with a large proportion of small firms, are sometimes given help in adjusting their structure of production. Nearly every major industrial country, for example, has had a program of assistance to rationalize its textile industry. And shipbuilding, railroad, steel, and coal industries have frequently received government assistance in adjusting. The textile and shipbuilding industries have received substantial help in the United Kingdom. But Britain, like West Germany, has also put substantial effort into programs to stimulate development in particular regions.

Sometimes technologically advanced industries, such as aircraft and computers, are assisted by governments to further self-sufficiency or to promote exports. Japan has had an especially strong program to aid in the development of sophisticated industries.

Finally, some governments, including Sweden's, have sponsored assistance programs for specific industries, but have also emphasized broader efforts to promote industrial restructuring and to train workers in new skills and aid them in moving to new areas.

The European Community

Adjustment assistance was one of the integration measures set out in the 1952 treaty establishing the European Coal and Steel Community (ECSC). The governing body of the ECSC was empowered (by article 56 of the Paris Treaty) to assist workers with compensatory wages, resettlement allowances, and technical retraining, and firms with loans to stimulate local employment opportunities. Normally, 50 percent of the cost was to be borne by the community, the other half by the member state. The adjustment assistance was designed to ease the dislocation caused by shifts in the location of production of coal and steel as the six member nations integrated their industries. Before the five-year transitional period expired, the adjustment assistance powers of the community were extended indefinitely.

Discharged workers were almost always given a "tide-over" allowance, usually lasting about twelve to fifteen months, which was computed as a declining percentage of their former wages. For example, an unemployed worker might first have been given 100 percent of his previous pay, then in successive periods 80 percent and 60 percent. Workers undergoing retraining were often entitled to assistance for an entire year plus a refund of retraining expenses. In addition, retraining centers themselves have received assistance. If a displaced worker was reemployed at less than his former wage, he could be compensated until he reached 90–100 percent of his previous wage for the duration of the tide-over period. Also, workers were occasionally given leave with full or nearly full pay when laid off because of plant conversions or renovations.

Assistance given for resettlement included reimbursement for travel and other expenses. Other special benefits have been tailored to meet particular situations. In Germany, for example, displaced workers were compensated for the loss of their entitlement to concessionary coal. In the same instance, lump-sum payments were made available to those workers who had not yet reached the compulsory age for retirement but were eligible for pensions. In 1974 alone under the ECSC's readaptation policy, almost $40 million was disbursed to more than forty thousand workers in Germany, Belgium, France, and the United Kingdom.[1]

The community's redevelopment policy has been designed to bring new jobs to the workers. The ECSC High Authority was empowered to give loans to individual enterprises in depressed areas in order to stimulate labor demand and the construction of workers' housing and larger power stations. Loans have been granted at more or less the market rates of interest to firms for coal or steel developments and at very low interest rates for the construction of workers' housing. From the outset of the program in 1954 through December 1974, nearly $2 billion in loans was disbursed under the redevelopment program to the six member states.[2]

The program of worker readaptation in its early years "proved to be rather unimportant, and not very exciting." In his analysis of the program up until 1958, Diebold found "much less call for community aid than was expected. The procedure has worked quite successfully in a few relatively minor cases; in one major instance it has not worked at all; and in another it has been applied in a somewhat strained and distorted sense."[3] Many of the unfortunate early experiences can be attributed to naivety regarding what could be accomplished in terms of relocating large numbers of workers, and to poor administration. For example, much criticism was leveled at the long time lag between the need for and the receipt of aid. As in the U.S. adjustment assistance process, a time lapse was inherent in the administrative procedures. First, the problem had to be recognized by the affected firm, and then those concerned were obliged to enlist the support of their government. Next, the government had to work out an agreement with the High Authority. Finally, the government had to arrange the actual operation of the plan. When procedures became more regularized in later years, the approval process was speeded up considerably.

The early years of the redevelopment program coincided with a period of labor scarcity in the community. In the late fifties, discharged workers could be absorbed easily, so the disruptions and dislocations that had been expected in the initial years of the community did not materialize. Most

1. European Coal and Steel Community, European Economic Community, and European Atomic Energy Commission, *Eighth General Report on the Activities of the European Communities* (Brussels-Luxembourg: Office for Official Publication of the European Communities, 1975), p. 122.

2. Ibid., p. 37.

3. William Diebold, Jr., *The Schuman Plan: A Study in Economic Cooperation, 1950–1959* (Praeger for the Council on Foreign Relations, 1959), p. 405.

workers tended to find new jobs by themselves, usually without retraining and in the vicinity of their old firms.

In the sixties, however, the pace of change in the Coal and Steel Community began to quicken. Low-cost sources of energy, particularly petroleum and natural gas, replaced coal. Mines began to close or modernize more rapidly. The result was a sharp increase in the applications for assistance and the number of workers helped. In the period from January 1960 to June 1969, for example, 276,000 workers were assisted by grants of $90 million from the High Authority, while from 1952 to 1960 only 115,000 workers were helped, receiving grants of $32 million.[4]

The ECSC integration efforts after 1960 can be viewed as part of the larger effort that culminated in the establishment of the European Economic Community (EEC). There unfortunately have been no serious attempts to analyze the effectiveness of the adjustment assistance efforts in the European Community since Diebold's study of the Coal and Steel Community. The programs have grown in scope, however, and the organized labor movement in Europe has pushed for their expansion.

One of the major institutions designed to facilitate adjustment is the European Investment Bank, which functions primarily to finance projects creating jobs in depressed regions within the European Community. The bank finances government infrastructure projects as well as private investment projects. From its inception in 1958 through the end of 1974 the bank granted a total of $4.7 billion. In 1974 alone the 84 loans granted by the bank totaled about $1 billion, two-thirds of which went to assist the community's backward areas.[5]

A second major institution, the European Social Fund, was created by the Rome Treaty of 1960 to alleviate the economic disruption that establishment of the EEC was expected to cause.[6] The objective of the fund was to help workers adjust to new jobs and maintain their income during this process of adjustment. Unlike the early readaptation policies of the Coal and Steel Community, the main thrust of the Social Fund of the EEC was to support retraining efforts.

Originally, the fund was expected only to assess applications for assistance and determine eligibility under the provisions for adjustment assistance. Its rulings had a redistributive effect, since member countries

4. Calculated from ECSC, EEC, and EAEC, *Fourth General Report* (1971), and earlier reports of the communities.

5. ECSC, EEC, and EAEC, *Eighth General Report,* pp. 39–40.

6. Broad outlines for the fund were offered in the Rome Treaty, arts. 123–28.

were assessed on the basis of ability to pay[7] and allocations were made on the basis of need. Fifty percent of all retraining, resettlement, and wage-level-maintenance expenses of workers who had been affected adversely by plant conversions were to be paid by the Social Fund, and the member countries were to pay the other half of these costs. The grants were paid directly to the governments for programs that they had organized themselves. Grants were given only after expenses had been incurred. Member countries themselves, and not the fund, were responsible for taking the initiative in setting up the various programs for assistance.

Workers in retraining received payments equal to 80–100 percent of their last annual wage during periods of unemployment. The only costs incurred by retraining centers that were reimbursable were the allowances paid to workers; since up to 135 percent could be reimbursed, member governments had an incentive to be generous with worker allowances during retraining. Compensation for up to two years was also offered to those workers who found lower paying jobs after retraining. Resettlement grants were made available to those who had to relocate in order to secure new employment.

By 1970, the tenth year of its operation, the fund had assisted 1.3 million workers with payments totaling $153.8 million, of which $145.4 million was allotted for retraining and $8.4 million for resettlement purposes. Workers in Italy, West Germany, and France received the largest portion of this assistance.[8]

In 1971 the EEC Council of Ministers, at the urging of trade unions in the six member countries, amended the rules of the Social Fund in order to broaden its scope and increase its powers. In addition to the 50 percent assistance granted to public authorities for retraining allowances, the fund was authorized to give assistance to private concerns for the same purpose.[9] Not only have such measures helped to soften the Community's own damaging activities, but they have been a guide for the member governments in dealing with their national problems.

7. The fund's resources were to be supplied by the member countries, in the following ratios: Belgium 7.9 percent, Germany and France 32 percent each, Italy 20 percent, Luxembourg 0.2 percent, and the Netherlands 7 percent.

8. UN Conference on Trade and Development, UN Doc. TD/121/Supp. 1, Jan. 14, 1972, p. 51.

9. Ferdnand Graun, "The European Economic Community Approach to Adjustment," in Helen Hughes, ed., *Prospects for Partnership: Industrialization and Trade Policies in the 1970s* (Johns Hopkins University Press, 1973), p. 206.

Canada

Canada's experience with trade adjustment assistance began with the Canadian-American Automotive Agreement. A specially established Adjustment Assistance Board[10] administered loans to automobile parts manufacturers and provided transitional assistance benefits to manufacturers and workers in an effort to assuage the pains of dislocations brought about by the elimination of tariffs.

Firms could apply for assistance if adverse shifts of production had occurred as a result of the agreement and their overall production was threatened with a substantial reduction, or if they would be unable without additional investment to achieve the scale of production required to compete under the new conditions created by the agreement. Loans for modernization and expansion were made available to those manufacturers who had a "reasonable prospect of a profitable operation"[11] but would not have had good prospects without financing. The loans were not particularly cheap; for example, the interest rate in 1969 was 12 7/16 percent. By June 1971 the program had been extended four times, and loans to manufacturers authorized under the program had totaled $94 million.[12] These loans were used almost exclusively to help firms producing automobile parts to expand exports rather than to compensate them for any injury.[13] The big automobile producers were not included in the loan program, since the tariff concessions that were part of the agreement were made largely for their benefit in the first place.

The Adjustment Assistance Board also administered a parallel program for workers in firms affected by the tariff concessions made under the agreement. Transitional assistance benefits were provided to automobile workers in firms where 10 percent of the work force or fifty employees, whichever was less, were threatened with layoffs of four weeks or more. The amount of assistance, which varied with the number of dependents,

10. The original board consisted of Professor Vincent Bladen, its first chairman, who had previously been chairman of the Royal Commission on the Automobile Industry, and senior officials of the Department of Industry.

11. UN Doc. TD/121/Supp. 1, p. 24.

12. Ibid., p. 25.

13. Klaus Stegamann, "Canadian Non-Tariff Barriers to Trade" (Canadian Economic Policy Committee, Private Planning Association of Canada, 1973; processed), p. 90.

ranged from 62 percent to 75 percent of the worker's weekly salary. The duration of benefits depended on the length of the worker's employment in the industry. Workers could receive benefits for as long as a year and a half, provided they were enrolled in a training program.

The automotive program was the precursor of a more generalized Canadian program of trade adjustment assistance initiated in 1968. Like the Trade Act of 1962 in the United States, the General Adjustment Assistance Program (GAAP) was a response to tariff reductions negotiated during the Kennedy Round. Like the automotive agreement, the program was designed to help those manufacturers who had been injured or were threatened with injury by the tariff concessions and to encourage manufacturers to take advantage of new export opportunities arising from the negotiations.

Under the GAAP program, manufacturers can apply for government insurance of loans made by private lenders, for direct government loans, and for consulting grants. They must show either injury or threat of injury from import competition, or significant new export opportunities arising from the tariff concessions; in addition they must have viable projects that require financing that would be unobtainable without government assistance. The General Adjustment Assistance Board, which is made up of staff members of the Department of Industry, Trade and Commerce, determines eligibility.

The most commonly used assistance is government insurance of private loans. An eligible manufacturer and a lender negotiate a loan. The lender may then apply for insurance on up to 90 percent of that loan, which the board may approve if it considers the manufacturer's use of the loan funds to be sound and workable. The lender is charged a fee for the insurance.

For direct loans, as for loan insurance, a firm must submit a plan to ameliorate its position that must be approved by the board. Direct loans are considered, however, only after it has been shown that a manufacturer has been unable to obtain a government-insured private loan.

The grants offered to firms that do not have their own consulting facilities and are unable to pay outside consultants are to be used in designing workable adjustment proposals. Firms may apply to the board for up to one-half the cost of these services.

Although the original motivation for the program was to assist firms injured by imports, during the 1968–71 period assistance was granted almost exclusively for government insurance of loans for export promotion. As of October 1971, the GAAP board had authorized loan insurance totaling $37.9 million, assisting thirty-seven manufacturers, and had approved $105,000 for consulting assistance to seventeen firms.[14] It had not authorized a single direct loan to remedy a serious injury resulting from import competition.[15]

Since 1971, when the GAAP regulations were amended, Canada has had a new approach to adjustment loans. Rather than placing the emphasis on individual firms, as in the United States, adjustment procedures are directed toward entire industries threatened with injury from imports. The first industry to be helped was the textile industry, with the passage of the Textile and Clothing Board Act in 1971. Under this legislation, companies can petition the board for injury determination. Along with their petition, firms are required to submit a plan providing for either the "continued efficient development" of their operations or the phasing out of production lines that have "no prospect of becoming internationally competitive."[16]

If the board rules affirmatively on the plan, it recommends to the Minister of Industry, Trade and Commerce action which may include quantitative controls and other forms of protection that are available only for a limited period of time. Protection must be terminated when the adjustment plan has been implemented or if the industry fails to follow the time schedule that had been agreed upon.

The GAAP procedures were also amended in 1971, and again in 1973, to liberalize the assistance criteria. Virtually any activity in the tradable goods sector is included under the new provisions. The amendments abolished the causal link between Kennedy Round trade concessions and injury. Eligible manufacturers now must either wish to restructure their operations so that they may become more competitive internationally; delineate new international trade opportunities in which a Canadian firm might compete significantly; or wish to adapt efficiently to competition from abroad that threatens serious injury. The principal financial instrument of the GAAP has been loan insurance, which by mid-1974 had totaled almost $41 billion.[17]

14. UN Doc. TD/121/Supp. 1, p. 25.
15. Stegamann, "Canadian Non-Tariff Barriers," p. 98.
16. UN Doc. TD/121/Supp. 1, p. 27.
17. G. K. Helleiner, "Manufactured Exports from Less Developed Countries and Industrial Adjustment in Canada" (University of Toronto, 1974; processed), pp. 39–41.

As a condition for receiving government guarantees or loans for trade adjustment assistance, manufacturers are required to give three months' notice of layoffs to both the affected workers and the Adjustment Assistance Board (when the layoffs involve twenty or more workers and will last two months or more).

Although not specifically related to foreign trade, Canada's policy for labor adjustment has played a role in the adjustment assistance program. Since the early 1960s, Canada has developed an extensive manpower program that includes training, income maintenance, and job placement.

Under the Technical and Vocational Training Assistance Act of 1960, the first effort in federal participation in manpower training, the federal government and the provinces shared training costs. In 1967 a markedly different adult occupational training program was introduced; the federal government pays up to 100 percent of the operating and training costs of the program, as well as the full costs of training allowances to approved trainees. Persons approved for training must have been out of school for at least one year, or have been in apprenticeship, and must be capable of benefiting from the course. Living allowances are paid to trainees with dependents and to single persons who have been in the labor force for three years prior to the training program. These allowances accounted for over 50 percent of the total expenditures of the program.[18]

Unemployment compensation benefits are disbursed under the Manpower Mobility Assistance Program, which began in April 1967. Unemployment insurance benefits in Canada provide for two-thirds of weekly insurable earnings (three-quarters for claimants with dependents) for up to fifty-two weeks. Weekly payments under the program averaged $68.45 in 1973.[19] Any worker eighteen or older who is unemployed, underemployed, or about to be laid off is eligible for a mobility grant under this program. Trainee travel grants are available for those who must travel to a training course far from their residence. Exploratory grants may be authorized for workers who are looking for employment in the closest area where there are good prospects for employment. The exploratory grant also includes living and subsistence allowances for dependents for a maximum period of four weeks. Relocation grants allow workers and their

18. Economic Council of Canada, *Eighth Annual Review* (ECC, 1971), pp. 101–03.

19. Helleiner, "Manufactured Exports," p. 43.

families to move and reestablish themselves. These grants cover transportation expenses of the worker and his family, a reestablishment allowance of up to $1,000, depending on the number of dependents, and a homeowner's allowance of up to $1,500 ($1,000 to be paid when the worker sells his home and $500 if he buys one in the new locality within a year).[20]

One of the key elements of the Canadian manpower program has been the development of local manpower centers which both employees and employers can consult for information about employment opportunities and trends. The objective here is to match jobs and workers effectively.

Worker adjustment was further eased by an important reform in labor legislation in January 1972 under which standards for advance notice of terminations by employers were established. The length of notice varies with the size of the firm, reaching a maximum of sixteen weeks for firms with more than three hundred employees.

Regional development plans also have been instrumental in adjustment policies. Under the Regional Development Incentives Act of 1969, financial assistance is offered to firms that propose to establish or expand their facilities in certain regions of the country. The amount of the grant is in part dependent on the number of new jobs that would be created by the investment. Firms receiving these grants are required to inform the Department of Manpower and Immigration of prospective employment needs and to cooperate with the department in its counseling, training, and placement operations.

The Canadian efforts at adjustment assistance have met with varied success. The most highly regarded program was that pursued in conjunction with the automotive agreement. The General Adjustment Assistance Program in its early years was not utilized as much as had been expected. Neither program offered much help for adjustment to import competition, but both facilitated efforts of exporting firms. The main factor limiting use of the GAAP was the strictness of the eligibility criteria; the 1971 revisions of the program widen the application of adjustment assistance. They also allow for more frequent quantitative restrictions on imports, particularly in the textile and clothing industries. The general manpower and regional programs may have helped adjustment, but have not significantly satisfied demands for special protection.

20. Economic Council of Canada, *Eighth Annual Review,* pp. 146–47.

The United Kingdom

As the oldest industrialized country in the world, the United Kingdom has long contended with problems of adjustment. It does not have a specific program of trade adjustment assistance, but rather a broad program of structural adjustment, which in many cases helps import-impacted industries, firms, and laborers. With the notable exceptions of the textile and shipbuilding industries, the British government has sought to cope with the problems of reconversion and revitalization of declining industries through either regional action or general labor market policies.

The effects of the decline of older industries have been particularly severe in certain regions. The government has had extensive programs of regional development since the Great Depression. Five broad development areas were designated in the Industrial Development Act of 1966, and in 1970, with the passage of the Local Employment Act, several other regions with less acute problems were designated as intermediate development areas.

To achieve an economic balance among regions, the British government uses both controls and incentives. Development certificates are required for new buildings over a certain size everywhere except in development areas. Certificates are issued only if the Department of Trade and Industry is convinced that the new venture could not reasonably be located in a development area.[21] The local employment acts, beginning with the act of 1960, and the Industry Bill of 1972 contain incentives for the expansion of existing industries and the attraction of new industries to development areas. Industries are offered grants and loans for building new factories and for training programs for workers, tax concessions, accelerated depreciation allowances, and investment grants for new plants.

Assistance for displaced workers in the United Kingdom is included in both manpower and regional development programs. Under the Industrial Training Act of 1964, the government established almost thirty industrial training boards to analyze the requirements of training centers and to provide training courses. The boards cover industries employing about 15 million people. They are authorized to give grants to approved training centers and to impose a levy on large employers within an industry for

21. General Agreement on Tariffs and Trade, COM. TD/W/152/Corr. 2, Aug. 14, 1972, p. 3.

training facilities, 90 percent of which is paid back to employers in the form of approved training grants.[22]

Under a program of regional employment premiums brought into operation in September 1967, employers receive a weekly subsidy for each employee located in development areas. The purpose of the premiums is to help increase employment in depressed areas. A labor subsidy will probably have a more powerful effect on job creation than other programs more typical of regional development programs, such as capital subsidies.

Transfer and rehousing assistance is made available to displaced workers under the employment transfer scheme of April 1972. The government also sponsors a nationwide network of some thousand local employment service centers at which employers register job vacancies and potential employees register their credentials and desired work. The centers also offer specialized services, including executive recruitment, occupational guidance, and youth employment. About 20 percent of all job openings in Britain are filled through this service each year.[23]

Worker security in the United Kingdom is affected by two major labor acts, the Contracts of Employment Act of 1963 and the Redundancy Payments Act of 1965. The contracts act, which was amended and liberalized in 1972, gives workers a legal right to notice of dismissal. The required notice, which varies with length of service, ranges from one week to eight weeks for workers with fifteen or more years of service. The payments act establishes legal standards for severance pay for workers with two or more years of service. For each year of service a dismissed worker receives half a week's pay for his service from age eighteen to twenty-two, a full week's up to forty-one, and a week and a half's to age sixty-five. Various limitations are placed on the total amount payable.

The redundancy payments scheme is partly financed through a government-controlled Redundancy Fund, to which the employer is required to make a contribution for each week worked by each employee. Firms may make a claim to the fund for partial reimbursement of severance pay; these claims have amounted to about 70 percent of the total costs of severance benefits to private firms.[24]

22. Ibid., p. 6.

23. *Manpower and Employment in Britain: The Role of Government* (British Information Service, 1973), pp. 6–9.

24. See W. W. Daniels, *Strategies for Displaced Employees,* broadsheet 517 (London: Political and Economic Planning, 1970), pp. 67 and 68.

To assist industries adversely affected by rising imports and other causes of dislocation, the British instituted an Industrial Reorganization Corporation (IRC) in 1966. The corporation, which was established by the Labour government, provided merger advice, counseling, and financial assistance. One of the notable mergers that the IRC was instrumental in bringing about was that between British Motor Holdings and Leyland Motors. The IRC was abolished in mid-1971 by the Conservative government.

A special program of readjustment was devised for the textiles industry. Between 1912 and 1958 the annual production of the British cotton industry declined by almost 75 percent,[25] principally because of the rise of Asian competitors. Surplus capacity and antiquated production and market structures characterized the industry in the 1950s.[26] Although attempts had been made by the British government in 1936 and 1948 to assist the industry, the Cotton Industry Act of 1959 was by far the most comprehensive legislation for assistance. The intent of this act was to reorganize and reequip the industry so that it could compete effectively abroad. The government designed two schemes to achieve these goals.

To encourage elimination of obsolete equipment, the government initiated a voluntary incentive scheme for scrapping under which two-thirds of the costs were borne by the government and one-third by the firms themselves through a system of levies. To administer the program, an independent Cotton Board was created. Between 1959 and 1966, when the provisions expired, the total cost to the government of scrapping obsolete equipment was $32 million.[27]

In addition, the scheme provided some assistance for those people who lost their jobs as a result of the scrapping of equipment. Compensation payments, negotiated by the trade associations and unions and the government, were based on age (subject to a minimum of five years of service in the industry since 1945) and average weekly earnings: workers aged twenty-seven to twenty-nine received three weeks' wages, while those sixty-five or over received thirty weeks' wages. Half of the compensation was available as a lump-sum payment; the other half was disbursed over a number of weeks and was adjusted downward if the former employee

25. UN Doc. TD/121/Supp. 1, p. 37.

26. See Caroline Miles, *Lancashire Textiles: A Case Study of Industrial Change* (Cambridge University Press, 1968), pp. 40–47.

27. UN Doc. TD/121/Supp. 1, p. 37.

found new work. Firms were held completely responsible for financing the worker compensation, but, of course, the scrapping incentives made it possible for them to offer compensation to workers. Over the 1959–66 period, worker compensation totaled $13 million.[28]

After the scrapping scheme expired in 1966, a Cotton and Allied Industrial Training Board was established to make training grants available to firms operating approved training programs. Potentially, these grants could be extended to some 250,000 workers in 8,000 facilities.[29]

The second basic scheme advanced by the government dealt with reequipping the industry. Eligible firms were required to submit plans for reequipping or modernizing mills over the period 1960–64. The government agreed to pay 25 percent of the costs of reequipment approved by the Cotton Board. Between 1959 and 1966 these grants totaled $38 million.[30]

The productivity rise caused by the 1959 Cotton Act was not great enough to check the long-term contraction in the industry. In 1966, quotas were imposed on cotton imports from almost all sources. In 1969 the Textile Council, which replaced the Textile Board, recommended to the government that the industry be rationalized and production shifted into those segments of the industry that were competitive. The council's main emphasis was on mergers and consolidation of existing firms, but it also advised that import quotas be removed and that depreciation allowances and investment grants be increased. The government accepted almost all the recommendations made by the council. The Industrial Reorganization Corporation was authorized to make $60 million in loans available to medium- and small-sized firms for modernizing, reequipping, and implementing mergers. By 1972, four vertically integrated firms in the industry accounted for almost half of spinning production and one-third of weaving production.[31]

The British government also helped the declining shipbuilding industry. In 1966 the Shipbuilding Inquiry Committee recommended that a Shipbuilding Industry Board be established to encourage amalgamation of

28. Ibid., p. 38.
29. Ibid.
30. Ibid., p. 37.
31. *Trade Adjustment Assistance,* hearings before the Subcommittee on Foreign Economic Policy of the House Committee on Foreign Affairs, 92:2 (Government Printing Office, 1972), p. 714.

firms and modernization of equipment. The board, created under the Shipbuilding Industry Act of 1967, was authorized to appropriate some $125 million for mergers, reequipment loans, and management consulting fees. In addition, the minister of technology could guarantee bank loans to British shipowners who wanted to buy ships from British shipyards, provided the Shipbuilding Industry Board was convinced of the shipbuilders' progress toward reorganization.[32] Between 1967 and 1971, when the act expired, six of the largest firms merged, and eight other firms combined into two groups.[33]

The British approach to adjustment has not been successful in halting the decline in Britain's competitive position. Many of the industrial rationalization schemes breathed only temporary life into industries that could not be helped simply by mergers, consolidations, and scrapping of equipment. In some cases, including cotton textiles, government programs were largely a response to pleas from special industrial interest groups.[34] Many of the measures were designed not to push firms in the industry to move into other lines of endeavor, but to reduce competition and provide protection.

The regional efforts also were generally not successful in creating a significant number of jobs in depressed areas. The programs were not geared to make labor more mobile but rather to bring jobs to the workers. There is some question whether this was the best strategy for Britain: because the decline of many particularly depressed areas could not be halted without more draconian measures, a policy aimed at moving workers out of such areas may have had more chance for success.

British policies have, however, provided workers with a great deal of economic security. In addition to increased unemployment compensation and improved health, pension, and retraining schemes, the English have been pioneers in requiring advance notice of terminations, in providing redundancy payments for workers whose jobs are terminated, and in giving lump-sum payments for workers displaced by government programs in the textile industry. Despite these efforts to provide economic security and to cushion the impact of economic change, the overall effect has not been to stimulate rapid economic change in the British economy.

32. GATT, COM. TD/W/92/Add. 6, April 30, 1969, p. 2.

33. UN Doc. TD/121/Supp. 1, p. 37.

34. See Miles, *Lancashire Textiles,* pp. 66–71, for a discussion of the cotton industry case.

The Federal Republic of Germany

Most of West Germany's economic adjustment programs involve incentives for industrial rationalization and regional development. Due to vigorous economic growth and labor shortages for many years, adjustment in Germany took place without burdensome costs to either business, labor, or government. Since the recession of 1966–67, however, the Germans have paid increasing attention to government assistance in structural adjustment. There is one minor program designed specifically for trade adjustment assistance.

The older industries in Germany have experienced the most difficulty in adjusting. The typical industry in need of assistance has a high proportion of small, relatively inefficient firms, each of which has only limited access to capital markets and consulting skills. In accordance with its policy of structural adjustment, in the late sixties the German government established a Rationalization Commission (RationaliserungsKuratorium der Deutschen Wirtschaft—RKW) to provide technical assistance to firms wishing to reorganize their operations. The commission, operating on a budget of $2.5 million a year, advises primarily small and medium-sized firms. The bulk of its funds is derived from dues contributed by member companies, and the remainder is supplied by the government. The commission disseminates advice and information on modernization, mergers, procurement procedures, joint research, marketing, and managerial and technical developments. The government also uses tax incentives to induce small companies to merge. Generous write-offs are offered—up to 50 percent on plant and equipment for research and development, supplemented by a 10 percent subsidy if the equipment represents a new investment. In addition, direct subsidies are available for joint research projects.

In Germany, as in the United Kingdom, much emphasis has been placed on regional development programs. The regional promotion program of the federal government coordinates the efforts of the federal, state, and local governments. The three broadly defined types of regions in need of assistance are areas near East Germany, regions where the economy is heavily dependent on a declining industry, and rural areas that lack industrial jobs. Investment subsidies of up to 15 percent of total investment for the establishment of industrial plants and shops are offered to firms in these areas. Typically, these subsidies are combined with low-interest loans from the Federal Office of Labor. In addition, sizable low-interest loans are available from the European Recovery Plan counterpart fund. Tax incentives, such as a 10 percent tax-free investment subsidy and a 7.5 percent subsidy for investments made for rationalization, are offered to firms in the less developed regions.

Until the mid-1960s Germany's low unemployment rate allowed for substantial labor absorption. A pool of migrant workers from the Middle East and southern Europe, which the German economy has relied very heavily on, has acted as a buffer. Fluctuations in the unemployment rate hit mainly these unskilled workers. Highly trained German workers have enjoyed not only a great deal of job security but relief from the very menial, as well as mentally and physically debilitating, occupations at the low end of the scale.

Since 1967 the German government has passed several employment, vocational, and training acts, including the Stabilization and Growth Act of 1967, the Employment Promotion Act of 1969, the Vocational Education Act of 1969, and the Federal Training Promotion Act of 1971. All workers are able to make use of German employment services, run by the Federal Institute for Labor. These services include vocational and job counseling, placement, training, relocation allowances, and unemployment insurance. In 1969, about $65 million was allotted for vocational training, advanced schooling, and retraining.[35] Although no specific legislation has been designed for trade-impacted workers, special attention is given to creating jobs and assisting workers in backward regions and declining industrial sectors.

One German program closely resembles the U.S. scheme of trade adjustment assistance for firms, however; it provides government guarantees and direct credits at reduced rates to small and medium-sized firms adversely affected by foreign competition, to enable them to shift their production into more competitive lines. Firms applying for the loans are required to present an economically feasible plan for restructuring their operations. The plan is forwarded to the government through the company's bank, which is required to review and comment on the viability of both the company and its plan. Credit lines are offered out of European Recovery Plan counterpart funds. In the period 1958–65, about $25 million was made available, although not all of it was used.[36]

35. OECD, *The Industrial Policies of 14 Member Countries* (Paris: OECD, 1971), p. 23.

36. UN Doc. TD/121/Supp. 1, p. 29.

The Germans only began to emphasize government participation in structural adjustment in the late sixties, and there have been no serious studies of the effectiveness of the program. Claims of success by the government have been directed particularly toward the regional promotion program, which is estimated to have created 10,000 jobs per year in the late sixties.[37] The trade adjustment assistance program for firms was hardly utilized, largely because of the existence of more attractive programs of government capital subsidies.

Sweden

Sweden, a country highly dependent on international trade, has no specific trade adjustment assistance programs. Workers displaced by import competition, however, are able to take advantage of a wide range of labor programs and policies which give Sweden one of the most highly trained and mobile labor forces in the world. In fiscal 1970, Sweden's expenditures on labor market programs represented 1.8 percent of its gross national product, or approximately $423 million.[38]

Measures to improve the geographical and occupational distribution of workers in Sweden are extensive. Many allowances are available to the unemployed and to persons threatened with unemployment. They include compensation for all expenses incurred when a worker and his family interview for a job, move, and resettle;[39] a lump-sum starting grant of up to $400;[40] and separation allowances of $90 per month for up to twelve months plus an additional amount for each child, to cover the costs of maintaining two households in the event that the worker's family is unable to move to the new locality immediately. The government also is authorized to purchase a worker's house in a depressed area if difficulty in selling his house is an obstacle to his relocating. As housing shortages often hinder migration to labor-shortage areas, subsidized building credits are issued to landlords on the condition that they give dwelling priority to re-

37. UN Doc. TD/121/Supp. 1, p. 30.

38. OECD, *Industrial Policies of 14 Member Countries,* p. 307.

39. Resettlement grants of up to $400 are given to families moving out of regions with high unemployment (GATT, COM. TD/W/92/Add. 3, 21 April 1969, pp. 3–5).

40. The amount of the lump-sum payment depends on whether the new job is permanent or temporary; this allows for the shortages in seasonal employment (ibid., p. 4).

located workers. In 1968, a peak year in terms of labor mobility, about 53,000 workers or 1.4 percent of a labor force of approximately 3.8 million received travel allowances, and about half that number also received some form of starting help.[41]

Retraining and vocational counseling programs are administered jointly by the National Labor Market Board and the National Board of Education. Participants in government-sponsored training programs who are twenty-one years of age or older receive monthly allowances, which vary between 40 percent and 80 percent of the average manufacturing wage level for male workers.[42] Subsidies are given employers who organize vocational training programs, the largest subsidies going to training centers located in areas with acute employment difficulties. In 1968, nearly 100,000 persons participated in retraining courses which lasted on the average about four months. The total costs to the Swedish government for training and subsistence payments in that year were about $9 million.[43]

Short-term labor forecasts based on information collected by local offices of the national employment services, combined with an advance-warning system, add to the effectiveness of Swedish labor market policy. Under advance warning, employers are required to notify their provincial labor boards three months in advance of planned layoffs, shut-downs, or increases in employment.[44]

As in all industrial countries, there are economically underdeveloped regions in Sweden which attract special attention. In the northern Swedish provinces, rationalization and weak industrialization of the forest industry are reducing the demand for manpower. The government supports the creation of local employment through temporary public works projects and subsidies covering a large part of wage costs.

Adjustment of firms to structural change in Sweden receives relatively little attention. Although technical assistance to small firms is provided through twenty-four regional trade development associations, individual firms are expected to make their own adjustment. There are exceptions to this policy, but even in such cases the focus is primarily on a whole in-

41. UN Doc. TD/121/Supp. 1, p. 34.

42. The amount is based on the size of the family and housing expenses (GATT, COM. TD/W/92/Add. 3, p. 5).

43. Ibid., p. 6.

44. "Swedish Labor Market Policy 1972–1973" (Swedish Ministry of Labor and Housing, Jan. 12, 1972; processed).

dustry rather than individual firms. The primary mechanism for industry adjustment is the Swedish Investment Bank (A.B. Sveriges Investeringsbank). It was established in 1967 to assist the industrial reorganization and structural adjustment programs and has $1.2 billion at its disposal to be used to finance modernization and mergers.

One of the industries that have had adjustment programs is clothing and textiles, which employs about one-third of all female workers in Sweden. Since the 1950s, import competition has caused a decline in the industry, precipitating a decline in the demand for womanpower. The Committee on the Clothing and Textile Sectors, which was established to analyze the problem, recommended that loans and guarantees be financed for rationalization and modernization of the industry. In addition, it recommended that provisional and transitional restrictions on textile and clothing imports from designated East Asian sources be used to favor domestic producers.

A royal commission studying Sweden's labor market policy in the early seventies concluded it has been successful. Among the confirming evidence is a sampling of 1,091 individuals who had received some form of starting help in 1964, 90 percent of whom had not returned to their former communities.[45] Another study, made in 1964, showed that among those who had completed training courses a year earlier, only 48 percent were employed in positions for which they had been trained, but another 38 percent were employed in fields allied to their training. A follow-up investigation two years later revealed that about one-third of these workers were still employed in vocations related to their training. The high fall-out rate was attributed to the chronic labor shortages in certain expanding industries, coupled with full employment. This was construed to mean that selection of applications had been limited to hardcore unemployables, so it was recommended that retraining be made available to other than unemployed workers.[46]

The emphasis on labor market mobility in the fifties and early sixties led to a high rate of emigration from depressed northern areas, which in turn led to sharp criticism of labor market policy by northern politicians. In the 1962 to 1964 period, the government began to shift its emphasis to measures designed to attract new industry to the north and to public works employment programs. However, the regional incentives policies

45. UN Doc. TD/121/Supp. 1, p. 34.
46. Ibid.

have not been particularly successful in attracting industry, and the public works programs have contributed little to productivity.

The combined effort of encouraging mobility and providing training, however, makes Sweden's work force highly efficient and mobile.[47]

Japan

Low unemployment and rapid economic growth in Japan have made special programs for trade adjustment assistance unnecessary. Japanese industrial policy, which is part of the country's economic growth policies, requires close cooperation between government and private industry. The basic objective of this policy has been to shift production and exports into heavy and chemical industries, which depend on technological skill to turn out highly profitable goods. To this end, the Japanese government has assisted in restructuring labor-intensive industries where productivity is low and technological expertise of little value.

Workers in Japan enjoy a particularly secure status. Under the traditional system of virtually lifetime employment, a worker enters an enterprise upon completion of his schooling and remains there until his retirement. Firms are required to provide retirement plans and health, unemployment, and worker compensation insurance. In addition, many firms offer a variety of nonstatutory fringe benefits, including housing, food allowances, recreational facilities, and private insurance schemes to supplement statutory benefits. One of the problems with the Japanese system, however, is that it discriminates against workers not employed in the organized sectors of the economy and against the self-employed.

Although the Japanese system precludes any real mobility of workers between firms, individual companies offer substantial retraining programs to prepare their personnel for transfer within the firm. Vocational training is also provided within entire industries and in public training centers. Those training programs given by individual firms or in centers established by associations of employers are eligible for public assistance if they meet certain legally defined standards.[48]

47. Ekhard Brehmer and Maxwell R. Bradford, "Incomes and Labor Market Policies in Sweden, 1945–1970," *International Monetary Fund Staff Papers,* vol. 21 (March 1974), p. 114.

48. See OECD, *The Industrial Policy of Japan* (Paris: OECD, 1972).

In addition to general assistance for small enterprises, Japan has had a few programs oriented to particular industries. The machinery and electronics industries, for instance, have been helped through special legislation to encourage modernization. Loans are available to firms in these industries through the Japan Development Bank.

The most ambitious assistance effort was that given the cotton textile industry in the sixties. After World War II the government encouraged the development of small production units in the industry through subsidization and protected the industry by reducing competition with mandatory industrywide cutbacks. In the early fifties, however, labor shortages and competition from both developing countries and domestic producers of synthetic textiles caused a decline in the growth of sales and in the use of productive capacity in the industry. In 1964 the government passed the Textile Equipment and Other Temporary Measures Law (the New Law), which was designed to mothball a sizable portion of the nation's spinning machinery. However, like the British, the Japanese soon realized that excess equipment was a symptom rather than the cause of the industry's ills. In 1967 the Provisional Act for Structural Reorganization of Specified Elements of the Textile Industry went into effect. The object of this plan was to modernize the cotton industry by replacing equipment and merging units of production. The Textile Industry Reorganization Agency was established to administer the program, to buy up and scrap obsolete equipment, and to finance new equipment.

The reorganization program for the spinning sector of the industry included fiscal and financial incentives to encourage small firms having at least fifty thousand spindles to join rationalization groups. These groups allowed member firms to retain their corporate independence while cooperating on marketing projects and coordinating production to achieve economies of scale. Taxes were waived or reduced for a given period of time for firms that participated in the groups, and the firms were given priority for low-interest long-term credits offered by the Japan Development Bank. By the middle of 1969 a small percentage of all target companies had joined rationalization groups, and those that had joined had realized impressive improvements in efficiency.

The weaving sector, with smaller and more fragmented units of production than the spinning sector, was divided into regional cooperatives which all weaving firms were required to join under the New Law. Each cooperative was obliged to design its own plan for rationalization, which was submitted to the Ministry for International Trade and Industry for approval. The goal was to scrap half the industry's obsolete looms and replace them with fewer, more efficient new ones. The Japanese government paid 60 percent of the replacement costs; local governments paid 10 percent in the form of low-interest loans; and the textile agency guaranteed commercial loans for the remaining 30 percent.

Adjustment problems in the Japanese textile industry have become increasingly difficult since revaluation of the yen in 1972 and Japan's participation in the voluntary export restraint agreement. Under a 1974 revision of the 1967 reorganization act the government set forth a plan to integrate the spinning and weaving industries into one sector and modernize the industry as a whole.

The coal industry's recent experience has been just the opposite of the textile industry's. With the energy crisis, there has been a resurgence of interest in coal as a source of energy. The industry is one of those that were expanded rapidly after World War II. In 1949, however, the Japanese began to encourage the importation of oil, and coal production reached its peak in 1951. Rationalization of the coal industry began under a 1955 law that called for scrapping excess production equipment. Despite intensive labor opposition, the abandonment of old mines was successfully accomplished in 1963 and 1964.[49] Even though the industry's obsolete mines have been closed, it seems unlikely that coal can be efficiently produced and used as a major source of energy in the near future.

There have been few serious studies of the effectiveness of Japan's adjustment assistance measures. Such measures, however, have been an integral part of the overall Japanese industrial strategy which is frequently credited with a major role in Japan's amazing economic success.

Conclusions

The adjustment assistance programs operated in other countries are extremely varied. The Swedes have emphasized income maintenance, labor training, and mobility. The British have tended to concentrate on income maintenance, assisting depressed regions and declining industries. The Canadians have emphasized assistance to new export industries, training, and worker mobility. Neither Germany nor Japan has extensive gov-

49. See Kiyoshi Kojima, "The Japanese Experience and Attitudes Toward Trade Adjustment," in Hughes, *Prospects for Partnership,* pp. 255–56.

ernment programs to help workers adjust, but the resiliency of both economies has made the problem of worker adjustment less difficult than elsewhere. The Japanese, however, have an extensive program of industry promotion and adjustment, and individual private firms have broad worker welfare programs.

A number of the programs reviewed in this chapter may have relevance for U.S. programs of adjustment assistance. The successes and the problems of the broad programs in Sweden and Canada emphasizing worker mobility and training deserve careful study. The exploratory and homeowner grants in Canada assist workers in looking for new jobs and in buying and selling their homes as part of a move to a new job location. Both ideas have been tried in the United States—the exploratory grant idea as a job search allowance in the adjustment assistance program under the Trade Act of 1974, the homeowners' grant idea as a part of the adjustment assistance program of the Department of Defense. Both concepts may deserve broader application in the United States.

The extensive worker welfare programs and the worker mobility within the individual firm in Japan are impressive. Though the techniques employed in Japan may not be applicable in the United States, their effects might be duplicated by a combination of legislated standards for treatment of workers and corporate tax credits for worker welfare and training efforts.

Nearly all the countries surveyed in this chapter have broad provisions for warning workers in advance of terminations. Firms receiving adjustment assistance in Canada are subject to particularly stringent advance notice requirements. The United States is one of the few countries that has no broad provisions requiring advance notice.

The British redundancy payments scheme is based on the laudable notion that terminated workers should receive a lump-sum payment rather than a weekly handout that terminates when a new job is found. As part of the United Kingdom's scheme for rationalizing the textile industry, terminated workers were entitled to a redundancy allowance, half of which was a lump-sum payment and the other half of which was paid in a weekly allowance for a limited period. The weekly allowance was reduced if the worker found a job. The lump sum is a way of providing the worker with compensation without at the same time creating a disincentive for him to find a new job. This kind of payments scheme and many of the key elements of other countries' assistance policies should be carefully examined for their applicability to U.S. trade adjustment assistance.

CHAPTER TEN

A Program for the Future

THE FUTURE usefulness of a trade adjustment assistance program for the United States depends on whether a general adjustment program, designed to assist those who are injured by economic changes regardless of the cause, is considered necessary. If it is not, a trade adjustment assistance program will be most desirable. But a trade-oriented program may also be desirable to use as the nucleus of a broader and more general program that is developed over time.

Trade Adjustment Assistance

Liberal foreign trade policies offer large benefits for many groups in the United States. Consumers can realize very substantial savings. Workers and firms in export industries stand to gain. But there are also victims of a liberal trade regime—the workers in import industries who in all probability will lose their jobs, and the firms whose sales and profits will inevitably fall. The benefits to many of liberalized trade may be much larger than the losses that some individuals must suffer. If this is so, then adjustment assistance is desirable to compensate those who might suffer from liberal trade policies.

The net benefits of a more liberal trade regime for the United States could be over $10 billion annually.[1] Even more important than the posi-

1. C. Fred Bergsten, "The Cost of Import Restrictions to American Consumers," in Robert E. Baldwin and J. David Richardson, eds., *International Trade and Finance* (Little, Brown, 1974), p. 132.

tive gains, however, are the losses averted in resisting protectionist pressures for a more restrictive trade regime. For example, the loss to consumers alone from the kind of trade policy reflected in the protectionist Burke-Hartke bill of 1971 has been estimated to be about $10 billion annually.[2]

In addition to these benefits there are nonquantifiable goals of foreign policy that have to be taken into account. Although trade relations with other countries are sometimes fraught with frictions and difficulties, their resolution often helps to strengthen political relationships. A growing interdependence through trade can provide incentives for the parties in a relationship to refrain from hostile political and military actions if they recognize their mutual economic stake in keeping it intact. A thriving system of world trade offers all nations a chance to sustain rapid economic growth. Access to the markets of developed countries is particularly important for the economic progress of the less developed countries, whose claims to play a more important part in world economic and political affairs are increasingly important in international relations.

Despite the very substantial gains that can flow from a liberal trade regime, such policies are open to attack. They are especially vulnerable to political assaults of those groups that are injured by liberal trade. Because those who are injured by import competition are identifiable groups who bear a severe financial burden, their influence on the governmental process may be more potent than the claims of a mass of consumers. For the benefits of liberal trade are diffuse and are not associated with an easily identifiable political pressure group.

Liberal policies are also likely to be attacked on moral grounds, and those attacks can be quite effective. For it surely seems inequitable for a small group to bear a severe burden as the result of a particular governmental policy when those who benefit do so only to a modest degree.

Both political reality and the demands of equity suggest that those who gain from a particular, easily identified governmental policy ought to compensate those who bear the costs of that policy. Furthermore, the costs of a program designed to compensate the small fragment of the total working force affected by import competition should be very small compared to the very large benefits that can be derived from a liberal trade regime. Thus a trade adjustment assistance program that is properly de-

2. Stephen P. Magee, "The Welfare Effects of Restrictions on U.S. Trade," *Brookings Papers on Economic Activity*, 3:1972, p. 701.

signed and administered should be sought, certainly in the absence of a broad and comprehensive attack on problems of adjustment. For unless some relief is provided for injury caused by trade, the political impetus behind the trade-restrictionist movement will grow.

The trade adjustment assistance program under the 1974 act is a very decided improvement over that in the 1962 Trade Expansion Act. Benefit levels have been increased. The legal framework for administration has been streamlined. The 1962 law was so restrictive that almost no workers or firms received benefits. The new criteria are more realistic and should enable many more workers to receive assistance. An imaginative new program of adjustment assistance for communities, not just workers and firms, has been added.

Not all the problems of the 1962 act have been eliminated, however. The incentives to encourage workers to find new jobs on their own or to move to new locales, for example, are not sufficient. If the 1974 act is well administered, however, potential exists for a much improved program of adjustment assistance. And the annual cost (estimated in appendix A) is not likely to be excessive—very likely it will be in the range of $250 million to $350 million, a small sum compared to the many billions of dollars of potential benefits from liberal trade.

A Comprehensive Program of Assistance

If government assistance to help in the adjustment to changing trade patterns appears to be sensible, then it may also be desirable for government to respond to disturbances caused by other factors. Changing defense requirements, stricter environmental codes, and high costs of developing domestic energy resources may cause significant economic dislocation that also calls for government adjustment assistance. It is not necessary to design special programs for each of these different factors. Separate programs result in duplication of efforts and a welter of different standards for assistance that in themselves are not equitable. Thus, ideally, a broad program of adjustment assistance, dealing with economic dislocation whatever the cause, is the soundest approach to the adjustment problem.

The existing, more general programs that might aid in the adjustment process are not sufficient to do the task that is required. Some community-oriented programs have been quite successful. But they are often either ad hoc, as was the Studebaker program in the early sixties, geared to a very specific cause of dislocation, as is the Defense Department program, or too diffuse in their application to have any serious impact, as are many of the programs of the Economic Development Administration of the Department of Commerce.

Existing programs that might help individual workers adjust to changing economic conditions are not entirely satisfactory. Not only are manpower training programs inadequate, but often they are used to deal with social issues such as high unemployment and school-dropout rates among youths or the problems of handicapped workers. Levels of unemployment insurance are not adequate to fully compensate most workers for loss of their jobs. Welfare programs help only a limited segment of the population and often not the working poor when they lose jobs. Supplemental unemployment benefits negotiated through collective bargaining vary considerably from industry to industry.

Some industries are noted for special efforts to help workers adjust. The meat packing industry's efforts are an example of success. The railroad industry programs, on the other hand, are noted for their high cost and limited effectiveness. But these ad hoc industry efforts do not constitute an effective comprehensive program.

A good program of trade adjustment assistance, therefore, is not so desirable a solution as a new, comprehensive program to help workers, firms, industries, and communities adjust efficiently to changing economic conditions. Within a new, broad program, however, it should be possible to identify specific groups that are injured by foreign trade. Trade adjustment assistance should not lose completely its identity in the more general program, but should be an integral part of a more general approach to adjustment problems.

An identifiable trade adjustment assistance program has several advantages. Trade adjustment assistance can be used imaginatively in conjunction with escape clause relief. The two techniques could often be used jointly in action to adjust to increased imports. If the two measures were seen as complementary, trade restrictions might be more quickly eliminated.

Trade adjustment assistance also could be made an integral part of a package of import relief measures negotiated under the General Agreement on Tariffs and Trade as an international code for safeguards. Such a code could also authorize quotas, or preferably tariffs, to ease the problems of an industry being injured by trade.

Neither a broad program of adjustment assistance nor a specific program for trade, however, can eliminate completely all protectionist pressures. No amount of monetary compensation can compensate some workers totally for loss of jobs. Individuals who have a stake in a specific institution—for example, union officials or the managers of a firm—cannot be compensated for the loss of power that usually accompanies the demise of the union or firm.

A broad approach should eventually be adopted to supplant the special program of trade adjustment assistance. It would include improved federal government social welfare programs, particularly a national health insurance program, further pension reform, and a reformed national unemployment insurance program. New laws would be needed to encourage the private sector to take more responsibility for assisting workers in changing jobs or location. And a broad community-oriented program of adjustment assistance would provide assistance for communities and workers and firms injured in those communities by foreign trade as well as other factors.

Health Insurance, Pensions, and Unemployment Insurance

A major problem for the worker who loses his job is loss of fringe benefits, particularly pension rights and health insurance. The loss of pension rights falls very heavily on the older worker. Full vesting and funding of pensions along with pension portability would greatly improve a worker's economic security and protect him from the worst financial consequences of losing a job.

Pension reform, however, is a complex and difficult issue, which should be evaluated on its own merits. It is not desirable that it be tacked onto trade adjustment assistance legislation, although the ability to carry pensions from one job to another, in particular, would reduce the injury caused by changing trade patterns.

The Employee Retirement Income Security Act of 1974 is an important step forward. This legislation mainly provides options that a company may choose among for vesting of pensions. It also provides for gradual funding of pension schemes, but full funding under this legislation will take decades.

The 1974 reforms did not include any provisions for the portability of pensions. Thus a worker must start from scratch under a new pension plan every time he changes jobs in companies that do not have a common pension plan. Understandably, lack of portability can be a significant barrier to labor's mobility.

Health insurance is a similar issue. Perhaps the best solution of this problem is to allow workers adversely affected by trade to join the federal government employees' program of health insurance. A general national health insurance program, however, is a better alternative. A program specifically designed for trade-impacted workers would be very difficult and costly to administer.

Unemployment insurance in the United States varies considerably from state to state in magnitude, in length of payment, and in rules governing eligibility. In some cases, unemployment insurance benefits are very low and provide only a fraction of most workers' former compensation. The inequities are so obvious that the movement of labor across state lines is distorted. More generous and more uniform unemployment insurance benefits would obviate the need for special trade readjustment allowances, except perhaps on a lump-sum basis.

Responsibilities of the Private Sector

Some of the burden and responsibility for adjustment assistance should be borne by private enterprise. It is possible for labor and management to cooperate in devising programs of adjustment assistance to ease the burden on the worker in adjusting to economic change, as the imaginative approach taken by the Armour Automation Fund Committee in the meat packing industry demonstrated. The United Automobile Workers and the Chrysler Corporation also successfully negotiated a special arrangement when Chrysler closed a large plant in Los Angeles. Older workers were given special early retirement benefits, and almost five hundred workers were transferred to other Chrysler plants with full seniority rights.[3] American Oil Company has been praised for the way it attempted to forewarn and protect both the community and their workers when it shut down a refinery in Texas.[4]

Large firms that merge or consolidate with small, weak firms or shut

3. See Douglas A. Fraser, in *Trade Adjustment Assistance,* hearings before the Subcommittee on Foreign Economic Policy of the House Committee on Foreign Affairs, 92:2 (Government Printing Office, 1972), p. 318.

4. *Wall Street Journal,* Feb. 28, 1972.

down plants should be required to assume some of the responsibility for assisting workers whose employment they may terminate. Government-subsidized assistance should go mainly to impacted workers employed in small, financially precarious firms that are not able to assist workers or transfer them to other plants.

On both equity and efficiency grounds, some of the costs of adjustment should be borne by the firm that terminates a worker's employment. The firm's ability to lay off workers gives it benefits, in the form of profits, that are higher than those the firm could achieve if it were required to retain redundant workers. If firms were obliged to pay part of the real costs incurred by individual workers and the government, their attitude toward layoffs would change and worker security would be improved.[5]

The private sector can share in the costs of adjustment in a number of ways. Any firm that terminates employment of workers in one plant can be required to offer employment to the workers in other plants before hiring new employees in those plants. Thus, no firm would terminate workers at one plant while hiring workers with similar or lesser qualifications at another plant. Furthermore, transferred employees could be given adequate relocation allowances, full seniority right, and flow-back privileges.[6] All fringe benefits, including vested pension rights, could be made fully portable for workers moving from one plant to another within the same firm. Unions could be required to provide portability of union-funded benefits, including pensions, for their members transferring from one local to another or from one union to another.

Any firm intending to terminate a worker could be required to give ninety days' notice of termination or full pay in lieu of notice. This would bring U.S. practice more in line with that of other Western countries that require notice of termination. In Sweden, for example, the Labor Market Board and the Swedish Employers Association negotiated a three-month advance notice plan. In England, a graduated advance notice scheme, legislated in 1963 and liberalized in 1972, gives workers advance notice up to eight weeks. Canada's scheme, liberalized in January 1972 and one

5. In industries that have adopted supplemental unemployment benefit plans as part of collective bargaining agreements, short-term layoffs have declined. As firms find they have to pay some of the costs of unemployment, there is less incentive to lay off workers.

6. Flow-back rights, pioneered by the Armour Automation Fund Committee, enable a worker to transfer to another plant but retain the right to full severance pay and other benefits if the new job does not work out after a limited time period.

of the most liberal, gives workers in firms with more than three hundred employees sixteen weeks' advance notice. An advance notice policy in the United States would shift some of the burden of adjustment from the workers to the employers and correct some of the gross inequities of the existing system of labor relations.

In addition to any pay in lieu of notice, terminated workers should receive a severance allowance. The United Kingdom's redundancy payments scheme is a good example of how the government can play a useful role in instituting an adequate system of severance pay. All firms contribute to a redundancy fund that they can draw on for severance payments when they terminate workers' employment.

Private firms can be encouraged to provide retraining and employment counseling and job placement services as the meat packing industry has done. They would receive tax credits for expenses they incurred in training, counseling, and relocating workers to other plants. A tax credit scheme would shift the administration of some adjustment assistance measures from the government to private firms, allowing the firms to recover the costs that the government would otherwise have incurred directly. At worst, such a scheme would cost no more than if the government were to administer benefits, training, counseling, and relocation.

In practice, however, it is likely to be much less costly for private firms to undertake to upgrade skills and place workers in new jobs than for the government to do so. For example, an unemployed middle-aged worker, who can be expected to collect maximum unemployment insurance benefits and many weeks of trade readjustment allowances, could cost federal and state governments $5,000 in benefits and administrative expenses. In addition, he might become a client of one or more local social service agencies, resulting in a further drain on public resources. If, however, the worker's firm were given a tax credit, it might choose to move the worker to another of its plants, at a cost of $1,000 to $2,000. Although this cost would be transferred to the government through the tax credit, the net cost would be much less than if the government aided the worker directly. The young new entrant who might otherwise have secured the job at the plant the worker was transferred to would be unemployed for a much shorter period of time, and he would in any case not be eligible for unemployment compensation. If this pattern is typical, the tax credit scheme would be a very efficient device for helping workers displaced by international trade competition.

Those firms and their officers and those unions that did not abide by reasonable standards regarding transfer rights of workers to other plants, advance notice of termination, and severance pay could be made liable for the costs of adjustment assistance to their workers incurred by the federal government. They could also be made liable for damages to the affected workers. The Department of Labor could be authorized to bring suit on behalf of the federal government and the affected workers against the liable parties. If, however, firms themselves incurred costs in readjusting workers, they would receive a tax credit. This would provide a double incentive for firms to assist in the worker adjustment process.

It is possible that some of the costs of placing strict standards on firms' behavior toward their workers will be shifted to the workers in the form of lower wage levels. But if this means greater job security for all workers, the costs will be shared by all of them rather than by the few who would otherwise lose their jobs when economic dislocation occurs.

A Community Approach

The community adjustment assistance program in the Trade Act of 1974 is modeled in many ways after the Defense Department program administered by the department's Office of Economic Adjustment. But it makes little sense administratively to operate two separate programs, one in the Defense Department and one in the Department of Commerce. In fact, a number of communities would probably qualify for both kinds of assistance. The same kind of program might reasonably be provided for communities hit especially hard by environmental controls or those that suffer from government actions in connection with the energy crisis.

An office of economic adjustment within the Executive Office of the President could handle the community adjustment assistance programs more easily than the Departments of Defense and Commerce. It could also initiate programs for communities affected by other forms of dislocation at the request of the President. A high-level focus on community problems offers the best hope for mobilizing resources quickly to relieve their economic troubles. Initially, a management and technical assistance team can be sent to help a community. With the interest and support of cabinet-level officials and the strong backing of the President, the team can act quickly, utilizing existing programs in manpower training and economic development and bringing resources to bear where they are needed most. It can cut bureaucratic procedures in the interest of mobilizing resources quickly. It should have its own funding and be authorized to make grants, loans, and loan guarantees to local governments and local private investors, much along the lines of the assistance authorized by the Trade Act of 1974.

The community approach has considerable political appeal. Community programs have often achieved high visibility. The kind of interest and concern that U.S. congressional representatives and high-level executive officials have shown in them can help allay parochial fears concerning the local economic impact of policies that are in the broad national interest. A congressman, for example, may feel freer to vote for legislation that is in the national interest if he knows that high executive-level attention will be directed toward local problems of economic adjustment which might arise, and if he can point to successful local adjustment efforts in the past with which he was identified.

Conclusions

The Trade Act of 1974 provides an imaginative new program of adjustment assistance. This program should be viewed as an experiment, with possibilities for more general applicability to assisting other forms of economic dislocation. Ultimately, the most sensible approach is a very broad and general program of adjustment assistance, designed to enlist the efforts of both the private sector and the government in facilitating the mobility of human and capital resources in mitigating the hardships associated with that mobility.

APPENDIX A

The Cost of Adjustment Assistance Programs

THE PUBLIC policy choice concerning the desired form of adjustment assistance depends very much on how the costs of various programs compare with the benefits they can bring. In this appendix the annual costs of an adjustment assistance program like that of the Trade Act of 1974 are estimated. The estimates are based on a simulation using data on whole industries. The simulation thus only roughly approximates the working of the programs in the 1974 act whose criteria for eligibility apply to individual firms.

The technique used to estimate the costs of trade adjustment assistance involves three steps. First, the factors that affect the degree of import-competitiveness of five-digit, import-competing industries are isolated, using multiple regression analysis. Second, resulting multiple regression equations are used to project the future degree of import competition by industry and the number of workers affected in each industry. Third, cost estimates for individual workers are applied to estimate the costs of adjustment assistance to workers. These are combined with estimates of the cost of adjustment assistance for firms to obtain estimates of total costs on an annual basis.

Explaining Import Competition

The degree to which each industry is subjected to import competition is a basic element in the estimation of assistance costs. In our analysis the forces that affect the level of imports are divided into structural and price factors particular to each industry, and general factors pertaining to the economy as a whole. The structural factors are those relating to the capital intensity, skill requirements, and technological characteristics of an industry. Price factors include the level of U.S. tariff protection for an industry, the level of tariff protection abroad, and the rate of price inflation in the industry relative to the overall rate of price inflation. General factors include the overall level of aggregate demand, which should affect the level of import demand in all industries; aggregate supply conditions or the level of excess capacity, which should affect the ability of U.S. industry to supply U.S. markets; and exchange rates and relative overall inflation rates in the United States and in countries that are its major trading partners, which should also affect the degree of import competition.

Our analysis is based on data on all of the import-competing industries at the five-digit level of the standard industrial classification for each of the years 1963, 1967, 1970, and 1971.[1] In a number of cases it was necessary to use proxies for single variables or groups of variables because of the lack of appropriate data.

The dependent variable used in our multiple regression analysis was the ratio of net imports to total supply, NETCOM. Total supply represents U.S. output plus imports. Net imports represent imports minus exports, a refinement that is crucial since most of the five-digit industries included in the analysis export as well as import. When the ratio of imports only to total supply was used, the results were rarely significant.

The first independent, or explanatory, variable used in the analysis was an indicator of the capital intensity of the industry. The first of three measures tried was value added per worker, which other investigators have used as a proxy for the capital-labor ratio.[2] The second measure was net value added per worker, which seemed a better measure than the first because the net value-added figure excludes payroll and is thus a rough measure of the return to capital. The third measure tried, the direct capital-labor ratio, is not necessarily the most desirable because of the

1. See appendix B for a description of import-competing industries and an explanation of the data used in the regression analysis.

2. See Hal B. Lary, *Imports of Manufactures from Less Developed Countries* (Columbia University Press for National Bureau of Economic Research, 1968); and Bagicha S. Minhas, *An International Comparison of Factor Costs and Factor Use* (Amsterdam: North-Holland Publishing, 1963).

theoretical and practical problems of measuring the capital stock. It seemed, however, to give better results as a measure of capital intensity than either value added per worker or net value added per worker. The latter variables were rarely significant, while the capital-labor ratio seemed to be an important variable in explaining differences in the level of import competition. Thus the capital-labor ratio, *KL,* was used in the regressions as our measure of capital intensity.

The second independent variable was a measure of the skill intensity and the technological content of an industry. Since it was not possible to measure the level of skill and the technological sophistication directly, a proxy was used. First we tried a measure of total payroll per employee, which includes both salaries and wages. We assumed that the higher the wage or salary level in an industry, the higher the level of skills employed and the more sophisticated the technology. But top-level executive salaries probably reflect implicit profits to some degree;[3] we thus tried a measure of total wages per production man-hour, which seemed to better reflect skills and technology. Experiments with the two measures showed that it makes relatively little difference which is used as a measure of skill intensity or human capital per worker. Since wages per man-hour, *WAGEM,* seemed to be less strongly correlated with the other independent variables, we used it as our variable in order to avoid multicollinearity.

Three price indicators were used as independent variables. The level of U.S. protection in each industry, *USPROT,* represents simply total tariff collections for the industry divided by the value of imports. The level of foreign protection, *FPROT,* is a weighted average of the amount of tariffs collected abroad in the industry divided by the level of imports by major trading partners of the United States. The relative rate of inflation for the industry, *WPI,* is the wholesale price index for a particular industrial category divided by the overall wholesale price index for that year.[4]

Aggregate demand and supply conditions, exchange rates, and relative

3. Wages or wages and salaries per worker have been used as a measure of human capital or skill intensity by Peter B. Kenen, "Nature, Capital and Trade," *Journal of Political Economy,* vol. 73 (October 1965); G. C. Hufbauer, "The Impact of National Characteristics and Technology on the Commodity Composition of Trade in Manufactured Goods," in Raymond Vernon, ed., *The Technology Factor in International Trade* (Columbia University Press for the National Bureau of Economic Research, 1970); and R. Bharadwaj and J. Bhagwati, "Human Capital and the Pattern of Foreign Trade: The Indian Case," *Indian Economic Review,* vol. 2 (October 1967).

4. A better measure of relative price inflation would be the U.S. price over the

overall rates of inflation in the United States and the countries that are her major trading partners were not directly measured. The proxy used to explain the year-to-year variations in the degree of import-competitiveness among industries due to general economic conditions is simply the level of overall manufactured imports relative to gross national product, *IMGNP*. When this ratio is relatively high, the ratio of imports to total supply is likely to be relatively high for all industries.

The structural variables we used to measure the capital-labor ratio and the skill intensity have opposite signs in the regression.[5] Ever since the Leontief paradox was postulated, studies of comparative advantage have shown that the United States tends to import capital-intensive goods and to export labor-intensive items.[6] Thus, we would expect the degree of import competition to be positively correlated with capital intensity and negatively correlated with skill intensity. We would also expect the level of U.S. protection to be negatively correlated with import competition, while the level of foreign protection should be positively related to import competition (when the net import measure is used since higher foreign tariffs mean lower exports) as well as to the relative degree of price inflation. The ratio of total imports to GNP should also be positively correlated with the degree of import competition.

Regressions were run on a cross-section of 207 industries for the years 1963, 1967, 1970, and 1971, on the cross-section of industries for each year separately, and on each two-digit industry over the four benchmark years. The results of the cross-section analyses, presented in table A-1, indicate that the Leontief paradox holds. At least in the import-competing industries included in the analysis, the United States tends to import capital-intensive goods and export skill-intensive items. Surprisingly, the level of U.S. protection, *USPROT*, does not have much influence on the degree of import competition. The coefficient is small and not significantly different from zero, although it does have the correct sign. The level of foreign protection, *FPROT*, however, does significantly influence the level of U.S. exports of items from import-competing industries. The relative rate of inflation, *WPI*, is also a generally significant factor in explaining

---

foreign price (for major trading partners) of the same category of goods. Data were not available to calculate this measure.

5. Similar findings are reported by William H. Branson and Helen B. Junz, "Trends in U.S. Trade and Comparative Advantage," *Brookings Papers on Economic Activity*, 2:1971, p. 323.

6. Ibid.

Table A-1. *Results of Regression Analysis of Import Competition in Selected U.S. Industries, 1963, 1967, 1970, and 1971*[a]

	Coefficients of independent variables[b]						
Industry and year	*KL*	*WAGEM*	*USPROT*	*FPROT*[c]	*WPI*	*IMGNP*	R^2[d]
All industries, all years	0.1322	−5.561	−7.601	0.3699	34.21	513.1	0.1065
	(4.24)	(−6.78)	(−1.40)	(2.63)	(2.88)	(5.99)	(16.31)
All industries, 1963	0.0790	−8.364	−8.881	0.0210	51.63	...	0.1443
	(1.32)	(−3.93)	(−1.27)	(0.08)	(1.93)	...	(6.78)
All industries, 1967	0.1246	−7.151	−8.024	0.1498	[e]	...	0.0923
	(2.14)	(−3.66)	(−0.71)	(0.57)	...	...	(5.13)
All industries, 1970	0.1136	−3.293	−7.325	0.6148	32.57	...	0.0855
	(1.72)	(−2.58)	(−0.49)	(1.99)	(1.26)	...	(3.76)
All industries, 1971	0.2556	−8.081	−11.421	0.4231	35.18	...	0.1279
	(3.40)	(−4.01)	(−0.65)	(1.19)	(1.82)	...	(5.90)
22. Textiles, all years	2.077	−4.520	−64.40	0.9037	...	−5.336	0.1799
	(1.84)	(−0.91)	(−3.29)	(1.29)	...	(−0.02)	(3.95)
23. Apparel, all years	−0.5270	−4.145	−27.35	0.3882	...	387.96	0.2209
	(−0.62)	(−1.49)	(−2.55)	(0.94)	...	(3.01)	(3.29)
24. Wood products, all years	1.397	−6.326	3.597	0.4588	...	554.36	0.1873
	(2.13)	(−1.73)	(0.12)	(0.94)	...	(1.97)	(1.94)
26. Paper products, all years	0.2335	−18.76	−898.7	6.688	...	624.38	0.8037
	(0.45)	(−1.11)	(−3.88)	(3.55)	...	(0.45)	(11.47)

28. Chemicals, all years	−0.0605	2.812	18.67	0.1051	...	89.20	0.1042
	(−1.23)	(1.38)	(1.82)	(0.27)	...	(0.49)	(2.19)
30. Rubber and plastic products, all years	1.481	−0.2343	23.43	5.924	...	582.85	0.9216
	(4.33)	(−0.13)	(0.78)	(8.11)	...	(5.10)	(42.30)
31. Leather products, all years	−3.248	27.32	87.64	0.7777	...	−634.32	0.4050
	(−1.80)	(2.17)	(2.49)	(0.80)	...	(−1.18)	(5.72)
32. Stone, clay, and glass products,	0.3995	−13.21	64.92	−2.426	...	1099.8	0.5206
all years	(1.96)	(−3.52)	(4.21)	(−2.66)	...	(4.43)	(10.86)
33. Primary metal products, all years	−0.0624	−0.7619	−45.12	−2.080	...	207.42	0.1507
	(−0.35)	(−0.47)	(−0.74)	(−2.37)	...	(0.70)	(2.34)
34. Fabricated metal products, all years	0.4548	0.9747	−50.80	3.873	...	−49.01	0.8139
	(8.03)	(0.44)	(−4.47)	(8.30)	...	(−0.35)	(29.74)
35. Machinery except electrical, all years	−0.7579	−6.829	−26.37	−0.6060	...	462.67	0.0977
	(−1.43)	(−1.64)	(−0.92)	(−0.77)	...	(1.40)	(2.30)
36. Electrical equipment and supplies,	−0.4397	−2.025	−1.849	−0.4529	...	356.20	0.751
all years	(−1.60)	(−0.80)	(−0.25)	(−0.48)	...	(1.66)	(1.40)
38. Instruments, all years	−69.39	−4.929	53.63	−576.35	...	730.64	0.7569
	(−0.21)	(−3.16)	(4.87)	(−0.22)	...	(5.07)	(21.17)

a. Based on 207 industries in the five-digit level of the standard industrial classification aggregated to the two-digit level. See appendix **B** for an explanation of the data used.

b. See text for definition of variables. Decimal points have been shifted two places to the left for all coefficient values to improve readability. The *T*-statistics, shown in parentheses, remain unaffected.

c. *FPROT* was computed on a percentage basis, while *USPROT* is a straight ratio. Thus, the figures for *FPROT's* effect on the dependent variable are only one-hundredth as great as the figures for *USPROT's* effect.

d. *F*-statistics are shown in parentheses.

e. Since 1967 was the base year for price data, *WPI* = 100.

the amount of import competition in an industry. A more significant variable, however, is *IMGNP,* the level of manufactured imports relative to GNP. Our analysis indicates that the most significant conditions explaining the degree of import competition are structural (the skill and capital intensity) and macroeconomic (which affect the overall level of imports relative to GNP). Price variables, in particular the levels of tariff protection and the relative rate of wholesale price inflation, seem to be much less influential.

The results of the cross-section regressions for 1963, 1967, 1970, and 1971 are quite similar to those for the four years combined, indicating that the results are fairly robust, regardless of which time period is used. The level of total imports to GNP is not included in the cross-section regressions for individual years since it varies only over time. This suggests that the degree of import competition in an industry relative to other industries is determined largely by structural and relative price factors, but that the overall level of import competition is determined by general economic conditions.

The individual equations for the two-digit industries vary considerably from industry to industry. The values of the regression coefficient, R^2, vary but they tend to be higher for individual industries than for the 207 industries as a whole. The Leontief paradox is not observed consistently for each two-digit industry. The capital-labor ratio tends to have a positive sign and the human capital variable a negative sign, but the level of U.S. protection does not have a consistent sign across the industry regressions. In textiles, apparel, paper products, and fabricated metal products, the influence of U.S. tariffs is highly significant and has the expected negative sign, but in the other industries the coefficient is insignificant or positive. The regressions for all 207 industries give much better results than the individual industry regressions. In the cross-section regressions, structural variables, pertaining to capital and skill intensity, and indicators of general economic conditions are more important than the variables referring to tariffs or relative rates of inflation. The lower significance of the tariff variables is probably not related to quantitative restrictions, since the U.S. tariff variable in the textile and fabricated metal industries, where quotas are the principal instrument of trade restraint, is highly significant. Instead, the insignificance is probably due to the fact that tariffs are generally low and that they do not vary a great deal across industries.

Estimating the Number of Workers Affected

In order to estimate the number of workers affected by trade, it is necessary to project domestic demand, the degree of import competition, and imports, exports, output, and employment for five-digit industries.

Domestic demand for the product of each industry was estimated as a function of gross national product and a time trend variable.

Projections of the *degree of import competition* for each industry were based on seven different sets of assumptions that use various estimates of the rates at which U.S. and foreign tariffs would be reduced, the rate of growth of GNP, and the degree of dependence of the economy on imports. The baseline projections for the years 1973–80 assume that both U.S. and foreign tariffs will be reduced to zero at a uniform rate over a period of ten years, starting in 1976; that gross national product grows at a zero rate from 1973 to 1975 and thereafter at a rate of 4 percent per year; and that the ratio of total imports to GNP increases gradually from 4.6 percent in 1973 to 7.1 percent in 1980. With this baseline set of assumptions, it was possible to make a baseline projection of the ratio of net imports to total production using the regression results shown in table A-1.[7]

To project *imports, exports,* and *output* for each industry, we had to assume that the ratio of imports to exports for each industry would remain the same in the future as it was in 1971. In combination with the projected values of the degree of net import competition and of domestic demand, this assumption enabled us to project the absolute level of imports and exports. Given our projections of domestic demand, exports, and imports, we were able to then estimate output.[8]

After having made projections of domestic demand, degree of import

7. Let $NETCOM_t$ be the ratio of net imports to total supply in year t. It can be projected as:

$$NETCOM_t = NETCOM_{1971} - 0.07601 \,\Delta\, USPROT + 0.003699 \,\Delta\, FPROT + 5.131 \,\Delta\, IMGNP$$

where Δ pertains to the change in the value of the variable between years 1971 and t. The coefficients are taken from the regression for all industries, all years shown in table A-1.

8. If $M/X = K$ and $Q = DD + X - M$, where M is imports, X is exports, K is some constant, Q is output, and DD is domestic demand, then we may estimate exports, imports, and output using the following formulas: $X = (NETCOM \cdot DD)/(K - NETCOM - 1)$, $M = (K \cdot NETCOM \cdot DD)/(K - NETCOM - 1)$, and $Q = ([K - 1 - K \cdot NETCOM] \cdot DD)/(K - NETCOM - 1)$.

competition, imports, exports, and output, it is possible to determine which of the five-digit industries would be eligible for adjustment assistance.

In the baseline set of projections made for the years 1973 to 1980, industries were classified as eligible for adjustment assistance according to the following criteria: imports must increase, and output and employment must decline. These are very similar to the adjustment assistance criteria of the Trade Act of 1974, except that they apply to individual firms, while our criteria are applied to industries.

To determine how many workers in an industry that qualifies for adjustment assistance will be affected, we first projected total *employment* in the industry by assuming a constant rate of growth of productivity for that industry over time. This rate of productivity growth was subtracted from projected output growth to obtain an estimate of the growth rate of employment.[9] Next we attempted to determine the number of workers in that industry that would be separated. We used an estimated separation rate for each industry based on the annual percentage of workers who are permanently separated from their jobs (it excludes workers temporarily dismissed who expect to be recalled seasonally or at the end of a short-term business cycle).[10] This separation rate multiplied by the esti-

9. The growth rate of productivity in an industry was computed as the average growth rate of the ratio of domestic output to employment for the years 1963–71.

10. Data were gathered on average annual gross layoff rates, new-hire rates, and total accession rates in each of the two-digit aggregations of the 207 five-digit industries that were classified as import-competing for the years 1958 to 1971 (data are generally available only at the two-digit level; the primary source for these data is the U.S. Department of Labor's monthly *Employment and Earnings*). In order to extrapolate the gross two-digit layoff rate to the five-digit level, we ran regressions at the two-digit level, using thirteen observations from 1959 to 1971, with the layoff rate as the dependent variable and the percentage change in total employment in the relevant industry as the explanatory variable. The regressions were run first using ordinary least squares, then using an autocorrelation technique (see Pheobus Dhrymes, "On the Treatment of Certain Recurrent Non-linearities in Regression Analysis," *Southern Economic Journal,* October 1966), and finally using ordinary least squares with a time trend. The latter technique provided the best results. We then substituted in the two-digit equations the percentage change of employment between 1970 and 1971 for the relevant five-digit industry and the proper time-trend variable for that period. These gross layoff rates included seasonal and cyclical layoffs. They were calculated by subtracting the total number of new hires from the total accessions for each two-digit industry for each month from April 1971 through March 1972; the monthly rates were then converted into an estimated monthly recall rate for 1971 (the total layoff rate for 1971 minus the estimated average recall rate between April 1971 and March 1972, assuming roughly an average three-month period between layoff and eventual recall). The separation rate was then extrap-

mated number of workers in the industry provided the estimate of the number of workers in the industry that would be eligible for adjustment assistance.

We also estimated the numbers of workers that would be eligible when the various rates of change were higher or lower than the baseline projection. Table A-2 presents the results of all the projections. With the baseline projection, the estimated number of workers increases sharply from 1973 to 1974 and declines rather consistently from 1974 to 1980. The highest estimate of eligible workers is 123,800, in 1974.

Variations in the rate at which tariffs are cut seem to have very little effect on the estimates. In this model, however, a high rate of tariff cuts leads to fewer job losses due to trade than does a low rate. This occurs because foreign tariffs are reduced along with U.S. tariffs, and foreign tariffs had a stronger impact on import competitiveness in the equation used.[11] Gross national product growth has only a moderate effect. The estimates are quite sensitive, however, to changes in the assumptions regarding the degree of overall import dependence—the ratio of total imports to gross national product. If we use the high estimate of this ratio, the estimated number of workers affected does not gradually decline: it reaches a peak of 140,700 affected workers in 1974 and averages about 71,000 the last five years.

The ratio of imports to GNP increased very rapidly in the early seventies, but it is not expected to increase so rapidly during the rest of the decade. The relative overvaluation of the dollar in the early seventies and an unprecedented worldwide boom resulted in a phenomenal increase in world trade. In the middle seventies the dollar was relatively lower valued and the U.S. and world economy were in a very serious recession, which tended to reduce world trade.

To provide some idea of the sensitivity of our results to the eligibility criteria for adjustment assistance, we made another set of projections using a more liberal set of eligibility criteria. We assumed that an industry was eligible for adjustment assistance if imports increased and employment declined, with no requirement that output of the industry also decline. These results showed only slightly greater job losses than those using the more restrictive criteria.

---

olated from the two-digit level to the five-digit level by taking the ratio of the separation rate to the gross layoff rate for the two-digit industry and multiplying the ratio by the five-digit gross layoff rate.

11. See table A-1.

Table A-2. *Number of Workers Eligible for Adjustment Assistance under Various Projected Trade Conditions, 1973–80*

Trade projections	Thousands of workers per year										
	1973	*1974*	*1975*	*1976*	*1977*	*1978*	*1979*	*1980*	*1973–1974*	*1975–1977*	*1978–1980*
No variation from baseline[a]	47.9	123.8	84.7	28.8	30.0	18.9	14.8	9.7	85.9	47.8	14.5
Variation from baseline[a]											
Low tariff cut (60 percent over 10 years)	47.9	123.8	84.7	31.3	31.3	20.6	17.2	12.9	85.9	49.1	16.9
High tariff cut (60 percent over 5 years)	47.9	123.8	84.7	28.3	30.4	18.9	14.0	7.9	85.9	47.8	13.6
Low GNP growth (3 percent from 1975)	47.9	123.8	84.7	34.2	33.6	22.9	17.9	9.5	85.9	50.9	16.8
High GNP growth (5 percent from 1975)	47.9	123.8	84.7	21.7	23.8	14.1	11.0	7.8	85.9	43.4	11.0
Low ratio of imports to GNP (5.9 percent in 1980)	47.9	99.9	78.3	15.6	11.3	10.2	6.5	4.5	73.9	35.1	7.1
High ratio of imports to GNP (11.8 percent in 1980)	47.9	140.7	112.9	74.0	78.5	68.3	56.0	79.3	94.3	88.5	67.8

a. Baseline projections: 100 percent tariff cut over 10 years, beginning in 1976; GNP growth rate of zero to 1975 and of 4 percent thereafter; ratio of imports to GNP increasing gradually from 4.6 percent in 1973 to 7.1 percent in 1980.

Table A-3. *Estimated Cost of Worker Readjustment Allowances under the Trade Act of 1974*

Trade projections	Millions of 1974 dollars per year										
	1973	*1974*	*1975*	*1976*	*1977*	*1978*	*1979*	*1980*	*1973–1974*	*1975–1977*	*1978–1980*
No variation from baseline[a]	89.1	230.3	157.6	53.5	55.7	35.2	27.6	18.1	159.7	88.9	27.0
Variation from baseline[a]											
Low tariff cut (60 percent over 10 years)	89.1	230.3	157.6	58.1	58.3	38.3	31.9	24.0	159.7	91.3	31.4
High tariff cut (60 percent over 5 years)	89.1	230.3	157.6	52.7	56.5	35.1	26.1	14.6	159.7	88.9	25.3
Low GNP growth (3 percent from 1975)	89.1	230.3	157.6	63.6	62.3	42.5	33.2	17.7	159.7	94.6	31.2
High GNP growth (5 percent from 1975)	89.1	230.3	157.6	40.3	44.3	26.3	20.5	14.5	159.7	80.7	20.4
Low ratio of imports to GNP (5.9 percent in 1980)	89.1	185.8	145.7	29.1	21.0	18.9	12.1	8.4	137.4	65.2	13.1
High ratio of imports to GNP (11.8 percent in 1980)	89.1	261.8	209.9	137.7	146.0	127.0	104.1	147.4	175.4	164.5	126.2

a. See table A-2, note a.

Estimating the Costs of Adjustment Assistance

The estimated number of workers affected can be used to estimate the expected costs of an adjustment assistance program under the Trade Act of 1974. The average duration of trade readjustment allowances under the Trade Expansion Act was about thirty weeks (see chapter 4). It is reasonable to assume that the average worker will receive thirty weeks of benefits under the 1974 act. Using the average manufacturing wage as a basis (about $180 in 1974), with the allowance under the new program of 70 percent of the worker's average wage, the gross cost per worker of trade readjustment allowances will be about $3,780.

However, the net cost will be much lower, since even with an adjustment assistance program, workers can collect unemployment insurance. In fact, the average trade-impacted worker received seventeen weeks of unemployment insurance while the 1962 act was in force. Since eligibility periods are increasing in many states, we might raise that average to twenty weeks for workers eligible under the 1974 act. Since the average weekly unemployment benefit was about $65 in 1974, the average worker would have received about $1,300 in unemployment insurance. Thus, the net cost per worker in 1974 dollars would be about $2,480.

In the last few years of the Trade Expansion Act about 10,000 workers a year were certified as eligible to apply for adjustment assistance, but only some 7,500 a year actually received benefits, since many individuals never applied or were turned down because they did not satisfy all of the individual worker eligibility requirements. The costs of trade adjustment assistance allowances estimated in table A-3 are based on the assumptions that 75 percent of the estimated eligible workers will actually receive benefits and that the average worker receiving an allowance will cost $2,480. To these costs must be added perhaps an additional $50 million for worker training, counseling, placement, relocation, and health benefits; $50 million for adjustment assistance to firms; and $100 million for community assistance. The total package would involve about $350 million a year at most, with $285 million a year a more likely average. This would be a small price to pay compared to the billions of dollars lost to consumers through restrictive trade policies.

APPENDIX B

Statistical Data

DATA used in chapter 3 and appendix A on output, exports, imports, and import duties are collected in U.S. Department of Commerce, Bureau of the Census, Social and Economic Statistics Administration, *U.S. Commodity Exports and Imports as Related to Output,* ES2-1 through ES2-13. The output data are based on data for shipments of products reported on the standard industrial classification (SIC) basis in U.S. Department of Commerce, *Annual Survey of Manufactures* and *Current Industrial Reports.* For comparative purposes, data on exports are converted from a schedule B classification and data on imports and import duties from a tariff schedule of the United States of America (TSUSA) basis to an SIC basis, as explained in U.S. Department of Commerce, *U.S. Foreign Trade Statistics Classifications and Cross-Classification.* The SIC classifications and groupings of data on exports are different from those on imports. Most of the data on exports and imports are reported on a five-digit SIC basis. Because of the problems of classifying trade data on an SIC basis, however, some five-digit categories are aggregated to a four-digit level or combined in four-digit aggregations. In some industries, particularly those for which there are *Current Industrial Reports,* data on output, exports, and imports are available on a seven-digit SIC basis.

Data are used in our study for industries whose imports were greater than 3 percent of total supply (defined as output plus imports) and exceeded $10 million for at least one year between 1963 and 1969. In addition, data are used for industries whose imports exceeded 5 percent of total supply and were greater than $5 million in value, those whose imports exceeded 10 percent of total supply regardless of value, and those whose imports exceeded $50 million regardless of the percentage of total supply. Data are used for 1963, 1967, 1970, and 1971. Wherever data for 1963 were not available, the data used are those for the earliest year before 1967 for which they were available. In order to make data on the various categories for the various years comparable, it was necessary to make further combinations and aggregations of industries, as defined by Charles R. Frank, "Industry Trade, Output and Employment Data," computer printout tables (1974; processed).

Trade data reported for 1963, 1967, and 1970 are from *U.S. Commodity Exports and Imports as Related to Output;* trade data for 1971 are from U.S. Department of Commerce, *U.S. Foreign Trade: Imports SIC-Based Products,* FT210, and *U.S. Exports of Domestic Merchandise, SIC-Based Products and Area,* FT610 (we cross-classified 1970 and 1971 data in the same manner and adjusted them to conform to the data in *U.S. Commodity Exports and Imports as Related to Output* for 1970). Shipments data on a product class basis are from *Annual Survey of Manufactures.* When data were not available for 1963, but were available for 1964, 1965, or 1966, the figure used for 1963 is an extrapolation of the annual percentage rate of growth between the earliest available year and 1967.

In order to obtain a constant price series, data on output, exports, and imports were converted to 1967 price bases. The data were deflated using the wholesale price index on a two-digit SIC basis; this required matching SIC categories with wholesale price categories in U.S. Department of Labor, Bureau of Labor Statistics, *Wholesale Prices and Price Indexes,* January 1971, Suppl. 1972 and 1963, and *Handbook of Labor Statistics,* 1969.

Data on shipments, employment and wages, and salaries were collected on an industry basis and converted to a product-class basis. For 1963 and 1967, data on shipments, total employees, production workers, production man-hours, and payrolls for all employees and for production workers, from U.S. Department of Commerce, *The Census of Manufactures,* were converted by prorating according to the ratio of the product-class output to industry output; they are reported for five-digit industries. For 1970 and 1971, data on shipments, wages, and employment on the four-digit level were prorated to each five-digit category on the basis of the ratio of product-class output to industry output; these estimates are reported on a five-digit, product-class basis. All data on wages and employment are grouped or aggregated in the same way as the data on trade.

Data on value added per worker, net value added per worker, and capital-labor ratios are from William R. Cline and Larry Hays, "Competitiveness Ranking and Disaggregated Industrial Trade Liberalization Effects" (U.S. Department of the Treasury, 1973; processed); these data are for the four-digit level. Value added data, from the *Annual Survey of Manufactures* for 1970, were based on the average number of production workers for the four months of March, May, August, and November plus the March figure for "all other employees." Net value added per employee was obtained by subtracting payroll per employee from value added per employee.

The capital stock in 1970 was calculated at the four-digit level. From the 1963 and 1967 censuses, book values of assets per employee were multiplied by the number of employees to produce the dollar book value of assets at the beginning of 1964 and 1968. The wholesale price index of finished producers' goods was used to convert the dollar value of assets and of capital expenditures in 1965–70 to real terms. The real value of assets in 1964 and 1968 and of capital expenditures in 1965–68 was used to estimate the real rate of depreciation. That rate was applied to the real capital stock in 1968 and to real capital expenditures in 1969 and 1970 to produce a figure for the real capital stock in 1970, which was converted to dollar terms by using the price index of finished producers' goods.

The level of U.S. protection was calculated as the ratio of duties collected to the total value of imports at the five-digit level. The level of foreign protection is a weighted average of foreign tariff levels on U.S. exports calculated in Cline and Hays, "Competitive Ranking," pp. 13–14, as follows:

The *Supplementary Tables* of GATT's *Basic Documentation for the Tariff Study* contain post-Kennedy-Round tariff levels for eleven countries or customs areas (including the U.S.). The GATT study aggregated industrial products into 119 categories. Because the height of a tariff of an aggregation of products having different tariff rates is an ambiguous concept, the GATT tables present rates resulting from four different methods of aggregation. We chose number three, which is based on a weighted average of tariff rates, the weights being each country's own imports. This is equivalent to dividing duties collected by the CIF (or FOB in the case of the U.S. and Canada) value of imports for each product category. . . .

Annex 1 of *Explanatory Rates to Supplementary Tables, Basic Documentation for the Tariff Study,* is a concordance between the GATT study categories, BTN headings, and SITC [standard international trade classification] product categories for 10 trading partners. Using this concordance we can determine tariffs on SITC product categories for 10 trading partners.

The next step was to aggregate trading partners' tariff levels into a single rate for each product category. To make our procedure more manageable we included only G-10 [group of ten large Western industrial] countries' tariff rates. The usual method would have been to weight each country's tariff rate on each product category by that country's share of G-10 imports from the U.S. We made the simplifying assumption that each country's share of each product category of G-10 imports from the U.S. was equal to that country's share of total manufactures imports from the U.S. in 1970, permitting us to apply the same weights to each product category. The results of these calculations gave us a weighted average foreign tariff level on U.S. exports classified by SITC categories.

To convert SITC data to an SIC basis we used a Commerce Department document showing the shares of SITC categories in 5-digit SIC categories in 1970. We used these shares as weights, which we applied to the tariffs on SITC product categories. This gave us a weighted average foreign tariff level on 5-digit SIC product categories.

To calculate the ratio of imports to GNP, data on real GNP were taken from *Economic Report of the President, 1963, 1967, 1970,* and *1971,* table B-2. Data on dollar value of imports for SITC groupings 5, 6, 7, and 8, which resemble most closely the industries in our sample, are from U.S. Department of Commerce, *Highlights of U.S. Imports and Exports, 1967, 1970,* and *1971* (FT990), and *U.S. Import Statistics, 1963* (FT110); they were converted to a real basis using the implicit price deflators in *Economic Report of the President,* table B-3.

The wholesale price index is taken from U.S. Bureau of Labor Statistics, *The Handbook of Labor Statistics,* table 130, for 110 product classes of widely varying aggregation. They were combined to the two-digit SIC level by taking a weighted average of product prices in two-digit classes based on indexes of relative importance reported in BLS, *Annual Supplement to the Wholesale Price Index.*

Data on imports from less developed countries were collected on a consistent basis for the years 1964, 1967, 1970, and 1971 (they were not available for 1963); they were taken from *U.S. Foreign Trade, Imports SIC-Based Products* (annual, FT210). These data were deflated to 1967 prices using the technique explained above to convert data on output, exports, and imports to 1967 price bases.

Index

Abel, I. W., 4n
Ablondi, Italo, 49
Accelerated Public Works Act (APWA), 83, 84
Adjustment assistance, general: broad approach to, 21–22, 152; factors leading to need for, 8, 150; government role in, 7–8; proposed private sector role in, 153–56; types of, 8–10. *See also* Communities, adjustment assistance programs for; Firms, adjustment assistance for; Industry approach to adjustment assistance; Regional adjustment assistance programs; Trade adjustment assistance
AFDC. *See* Aid to families with dependent children
AFDC-UF. *See* Aid to families with dependent children—unemployed father
AFL-CIO, 4–5, 16, 36–37
Africa, 33, 34, 36
Aid to families with dependent children (AFDC), 91, 97
Aid to families with dependent children —unemployed father (AFDC-UF), 96–97, 99
Amalgamated Meat Cutters and Butcher Workmen of North America, 117
Amtrak, 114, 115, 122
Appalachia, 83, 84–86, 88
Appalachian Regional Commission, 85–86, 88
Appalachian Regional Development Act of *1965*, 84
Area Redevelopment Act (ARA), 83, 84
Area Redevelopment Administration, 83, 86. *See also* Economic Development Administration (EDA)
Armour and Company, 65; automation fund, 118, 119, 123, 153, 154n; displaced workers in, 116–17; interplant transfer program, 118, 119, 121; plant closings, 116; retraining of workers by, 118, 119, 121; subsistence allowance to workers, 121
Asia, 33, 34, 36
Automation. *See* Technological improvements
Automotive Agreement Adjustment Board, 55–56, 57
Automotive industry. *See* Automotive Products Trade Act of *1965*; Canadian-American Automotive Agreement
Automotive Products Trade Act of *1965*, 3, 40, 55, 56, 57

Baldwin, Robert E., 5n, 13n, 14, 148n
Barger, Harold, 110n
Bayh, Birch, 80
Bedell, Catherine, 49
Beigie, Carl E., 40n
Bell Report, 2
Bergsten, C. Fred, 5n, 13, 14, 15, 16, 17n, 115n, 148n
Bernstein, Merton C., 104n
Bladen, Vincent, 129n
Blitz, Herbert J., 101n, 106n, 108n
Brademas, John, 80, 82
Bradford, Maxwell R., 144n
Brehmer, Ekhard, 144n
Brotherhood of Locomotive Firemen and Enginemen, 112, 113
Brotherhood of Railroad Trainmen, 111
Bureau of Labor Statistics, 104, 106
Burke-Hartke bill, 15, 16, 149
Burke, James, 16
Business community, 1, 3, 153–55

Canada: adjustment assistance to automotive industry, 9, 39, 129–30; aid to textile industry, 131; duty remission plan, 39; general trade adjustment assistance program, 130–33; manpower programs, 132–33; move of Studebaker facility to, 79; railroad employment agreements, 112–13; regional development plan, 133; required advance notice of employment termination, 102, 132, 147, 155–56
Canadian-American Automotive Agreement, 9, 57, 62; provisions of, 39–40, 129. *See also* Automotive Products Trade Act of *1965*
Canadian Pacific Railroad, 113
Cheh, John H., 14n
Chrysler Corporation, 153
Clubb, Bruce E., 48
Coal industry, European, 9, 125–27
Collective bargaining: advance notice for plant closings or relocation through, 100–02, 119; in meat packing industry, 117, 118–19; pension plan provisions through, 103–06; in railroad industry, 111–15; severance pay provisions through, 102–03, 119; SUB plan negotiations and, 98–99; wage-employment guarantees from, 99, 100
Commerce, Department of, 58, 72; certification for adjustment assistance eligibility, 41, 49, 51; monitoring system for economic data, 68; technical assistance by, 44. *See also* Area Redevelopment Administration; Economic Development Administration (EDA)
Communities, adjustment assistance programs for, 9–10, 66; benefits from, 78, 79; coordination of, 72, 156–57; in Europe, 126–27; evaluation of, 150–51; extent of, 77; factors leading to need for, 73; job development and, 76; problems relating to, 78–79; proposals for future, 152, 156–57; relocation of workers through, 77; in South Bend, 79–82; technical assistance through, 75–76
Compensation principle, 12–13, 19
Comprehensive Employment and Training Act of *1973*, 93
Computer industry, France, 9
Conference of Appalachian Governors, 84
Congress, 66, 68, 78. *See also* House of Representatives; Senate
Consumers, 13–14, 149
Contracts of Employment Act of *1963* (United Kingdom), 102 135
Costs: adjustment, 14; of import restrictions, 13–15, 149; of regulating firms' behavior toward workers, 156; social, 10, 14
Countervailing duties, 39
Culver, John C., 5
Cumberland, John H., 86n
Cushman, Edward L., 118n

Daniels, W. W., 135n
Defense contracts, cutbacks in, 72; aid to workers affected by, 68, 77; as cause of economic dislocation, 73; delayed announcements of, 78–79
Defense, Department of, 66, 68, 77, 147. *See also* Office of Economic Adjustment (OEA)
Demand, domestic, effect on employment, 27–28
Diebold, William, Jr., 126
Displaced workers: in Appalachia, 83, 84; in European coal and steel industries, 125–26; in meat packing industry, 116, 117, 118; in railroad industry, 111, 112; in Sweden, 141; in United Kingdom, 135
Douglas, Paul, 89

Economic Development Administration (EDA), 72, 82, 151; administration of regional development programs, 84; community adjustment assistance programs, 76, 87, 156; creation of, 86; evaluation of programs of, 88, 89; types of assistance provided by, 87
Economic dislocation: from defense cutbacks, 73; factors leading to, 21–22; forms of government intervention to alleviate, 7–8; from military base closings, 73; from plant closings, 79–80, 116–17; in United Kingdom, 136–37
Economic Opportunity Act of *1964*, 93, 94
ECSC. *See* European Coal and Steel Community
EDA. *See* Economic Development Administration
EEC. *See* European Economic Community

Egmand, Michael R., 46, 47n
Eisenhower, Dwight D., 113
Electrical workers' union, 16, 20
Emergency Railroad Transportation Act (*1933*), 111
Employee Retirement Income Security Act of *1974* (ERISA), 105, 152
Employment: advance notice of termination of, 100–02, 154, 155–56; effect of domestic demand on, 28; effect of labor productivity on, 28, 30; impact of less developed countries on, 34, 36; impact of trade on, 23, 27–28, 30–31, 33, 36–37; in import-competing industries, 24, 28. *See also* Employment potential; Employment services; Unemployment; Workers
Employment potential, 27, 30–31, 36
Employment Promotion Act of *1969* (West Germany), 140
Employment services, 8; community-action, 94; federal-state system for, 93, 94; under Trade Expansion Act, 1, 58; in West Germany, 140
Environmental standards, 8, 110
ERISA. *See* Employee Retirement Income Security Act of *1974*
Escape clause relief, 1–2; eligibility criteria for, 40, 60; on industry basis, 62; for piano and piano parts industry, 45, 49; Tariff Commission findings on, 41; under Trade Act of *1974*, 60, 61, 62; under Trade Expansion Act, 39, 40, 49
European Coal and Steel Community (ECSC), 9, 125–27
European Economic Community (EEC), 127, 128
European Investment Bank, 127
European Social Fund, 127–28
Executive Office of the President, 156
Exports, 24, 27, 28

Faber, Seymour, 65n
Fahey, Frank J., 80n
Federal Housing Administration, 77
Federal Railroad Retirement Board, 95
Federal Training Promotion Act of *1971* (West Germany), 140
Feldstein, Martin S., 67n
Ferman, Louis A., 65n
Firms, adjustment assistance for, 9; private sector responsibility for, 153–56; for replacing obsolete equipment, 136–37; through technical assistance, 12, 64; under Trade Act of *1974*, 64; under Trade Expansion Act, 41, 42–43, 49–53, 61–62; types of, 1, 64
Food stamp program, 9, 97, 99
Fooks, Marvin, 53n, 57n
Ford Motor Company, 98
Foreign trade: benefits from liberal policy for, 13–14, 15, 149; impact on employment, 23, 27; industry variations in volume of, 24; political opposition to liberal policy for, 15–16, 18, 149
France, 9, 128
Frank, Charles R., Jr., 5n
Franke, Walter H., 65n, 118n
Fraser, Douglas A., 115n, 153n
Fringe benefits, 108, 114, 152, 154
Fulton, Joseph F., 114n

GAAP. *See* General Adjustment Assistance Program
GATT. *See* General Agreement on Tariffs and Trade
General Adjustment Assistance Program (GAAP) (Canada), 130–33
General Agreement on Tariffs and Trade (GATT), 1, 151
Germany. *See* West Germany
Goldstein, Jon H., 92n
Grants: Canadian adjustment assistance, 130, 132–33; European Social Fund, 128; for job development and training, 75; for public works, 10, 76, 83, 87; subsistence, 121; supplemental, 85, 87; to United Kingdom training centers, 134–35, 137
Graun, Ferdnand, 128n

Haber, William, 65n
Hartke, Vance, 15, 80
Health, Education, and Welfare, Department of, 72
Health insurance, 9, 108, 153
Helleiner, G. K., 131n, 132n
Henle, Peter, 8n
Highway development programs, 85, 86
Hollister, Robinson G., 95n
Holt, Charles C., 94n
House of Representatives: Committee on Foreign Affairs Subcommittee on Foreign Economic Policy, 4n, 5; Ways and Means Committee, 5, 70
Housing and Urban Development, Department of, 72, 76
Hughes, Helen, 13n, 128n

Imports: of cotton textiles, 30; impact on employment of, 23, 30–31; indirect effects of changes in, 28; from less developed countries, 33, 34; net, 24; of paper and paper products, 30; rate of growth of, 27; restrictions on, 1–2, 13–15, 18. *See also* Industries, import-competing
Income maintenance programs: through AFDC payments, 97; effects of, 94; evaluation of, 108–09; through food stamps, 97; in Sweden, 141–42; through unemployment compensation, 95
Income redistribution, 20
Industrial Reorganization Corporation (IRC) (United Kingdom), 136, 137
Industries, import-competing: effect of less developed countries on, 33; employment in, 27–28, 33; percentage of total output and employment by, 23, 24; productivity in, 30
Industry approach to adjustment assistance, 8, 9; for automotive industry, 39, 129–31; for coal and steel industries, 9, 125–27; in Japan, 9, 144; for meat packing industry, 115–22; for railroad industry, 110–15; for textile industry, 131
Inflation, 15
Insurance, government, 7–8, 11
International Labour Office, 37
Interstate Commerce Commission, 112
Isard, Peter, 30
Italy, 128

Japan, 9, 144–46, 147
Japan Development Bank, 145
Job Corps, 91, 92, 93, 94
Job Opportunities in the Business Sector (JOBS), 91, 92
Job search allowance, 67, 147
Johnson, Lyndon B., 4, 80, 82
Jonish, James, 57n

Kennedy, John F., 83, 84
Kennedy Round, 1, 46, 47, 131
Kojima, Kiyoshi, 146n
Krause, Lawrence B., 16n, 31

Labor, Department of, 58, 72, 156; assistance to South Bend, 81; certification for adjustment assistance eligibility, 41, 43, 53; manpower training programs, 45, 67, 75, 91; monitoring system for economic data, 68; Project ABLE, 81; survey of workers receiving adjustment assistance, 54–55
Labor unions: attitude toward liberal trade policies, 4–5, 16, 17, 19; effect of trade policy on membership of, 16, 20; opposition to multinational corporations, 18, 20; reaction to adjustment assistance programs, 1, 3, 4–5
Latin America, 33, 34, 36
Laudicina, Paul A., 19n
LDCs. *See* Less developed countries
Lefcowitz, Myron J., 95n
Leonard, William, 49
Less developed countries (LDCs), 15, 33, 34, 36
Levitan, Sar, 83n
Loans and loan guarantees: amount of, 52; under Canadian adjustment assistance program, 129, 130, 131; to depressed areas, 87, 127; to firms, 1, 9, 12, 44, 52, 64; for meat packing industry workers, 117, 121; for Swedish textile industry, 143; under two-tier adjustment assistance system, 70

McDonald, David, 3
Magee, Stephen P., 13, 14, 15, 149n
Mangum, Garth L., 92n
Manley, Jeffrey A., 56n
Manpower Development and Training Act (MDTA), 94, 119; benefits under, 44; number enrolled under, 91; program in South Bend, 81; success of programs under, 93
Manpower Mobility Assistance Program (Canada), 132
Manpower training, foreign: allowances for, 128; in Canada, 132; for European coal and steel workers, 125; in Japan, 144; in Sweden, 142; in United Kingdom, 134–35
Manpower training, U.S., 8; under Comprehensive Employment and Training Act of *1973*, 93; under Economic Opportunity Act of *1964*, 91; under EDA program, 89; effect on employment, 94; evaluation of programs, 91–93; under MDTA, 44, 81, 91, 92, 93, 119; for meat packing industry workers, 117, 118, 119; on-the-job, 91, 92; by private sector, 90, 91, 155; for railroad workers, 115; South Bend program for, 81, 82, 89; under Trade Act of

1974, 67; under Trade Expansion Act, 44–45, 58, 67
Manufacturing industries: impact of trade on employment in, 27–28, 30–31, 33; import-competing, 23–24
Mathieson, John A., 31n
MDTA. *See* Manpower Development and Training Act
Meany, George, 5
Meat Import Act, 15
Meat packing industry, 115–22, 151, 155. *See also* Armour and Company
Metzger, Stanley D., 2, 3n
Michelman, Kathryn, 97n
Miles, Caroline, 136n, 138n
Military base closings, 72–79
Mills bill, 5, 15
Minchew, Daniel, 49
Mintz, Ilse, 13
Mirengoff, William, 93n
Moore, George M., 48, 49
Multinational corporations, 11, 17, 19n; labor and, 18, 20; Trade Act of *1974* provisions relating to, 63
Munts, Raymond, 95n
Murray, Tracy W., 46, 47n
Mutti, John H., 13, 14

Neighborhood Youth Corps, 91, 92, 94
Nelson, James C., 111n, 113n
Nixon, Richard M., 5, 16, 60, 96
Norway, 8

Office of Economic Adjustment (OEA): community adjustment assistance program, 76, 77–78, 156; functions of, 72–73; problems relating to assistance programs of, 78–79
Office of Economic Opportunity, 73
Orr, Larry L., 95n
Output, industrial, 23, 24, 27–28

Paidar, Emil J., Company, 52
Palen, J. John, 80n
Paper and paper products industry, 30
Paris Treaty, 125
Parker, Joseph, 49
Payroll tax, 96
Pension plans, 9, 103, 109; early retirement option in, 104; for meat packing industry, 118; portability of, 106, 152–53, 154; proposed funding reforms for, 105–06; for railroad workers, 115; vesting provisions in, 105, 152
Piano and piano parts industry, 45, 49
Presidential Railroad Commission (*1960*), 113
Production, industrial, 23, 24, 27–28
Productivity, labor, 28, 30, 33, 111
Project ABLE, 81
Protectionism, 13–14, 15–16, 18–19
Public Works and Economic Development Act of *1965*, 84, 86, 87–88

Railroad industry: adjustment assistance for, 115, 151; decline in employment in, 110–11; dispute over firemen's employment in, 113–14; employee protective guarantees in, 111–12, 114–15; government role in reorganizing, 12
Railroad Retirement Fund, 115
Randall Commission Report, 3
Readjustment allowance: cost of, 155; eligibility for, 42, 53–54; in meat packing industry, 119, 121; in railroad industry, 112. *See also* Relocation of workers
Redundancy Payments Act of *1965* (United Kingdom), 135
Regional adjustment assistance programs, 9–10, 82; in Appalachia, 85–86; in Canada, 133; EDA administration of, 86–88; legislation providing for, 83–84; multistate, 88; in Sweden, 142; in United Kingdom, 134–35; in West Germany, 139–40
Regional Development Incentives Act of *1969* (Canada), 133
Relocation of workers: advance notice of, 100–02; allowances for, 1, 3, 42, 45, 67–68, 119, 132; assistance to communities for, 77; from European coal and steel industries, 125; homeowners' assistance and, 77, 132; in Sweden, 141, 143
Resources allocation, 8, 12
Retirement. *See* Pension plans
Reuther, Walter, 3
Richardson, J. David, 5n, 13n, 148n
Richardson, Joe, 97n
Rindler, Lester, 93n
Robin, Gerald D., 92n
Rome Treaty, 127
Ross, Irwin, 5n, 16n, 23n
Rothblatt, Donald N., 83n
Ruttenberg, Stanley H., 4n, 23n

Samuelson, Paul A., 17
Senate: Finance Committee, 5, 70
Service industries, 16–17

Severance pay, 109; amount of, 102–03; government role in instituting system for, 155; in lieu of advance notice, 102; for meat packing industry workers, 118; for railroad workers, 114
Sewell, David O., 92n
Sheppard, Harold L., 65n
Shipbuilding Industry Act of *1967* (United Kingdom), 138
Shipbuilding industry, United Kingdom, 137–38
Shoe industry, 53, 62
Shultz, George P., 65n, 116n, 118n
SIC. *See* Standard industrial classification
Small Business Administration, 73, 75
Somers, Gerald G., 118n
South Bend, 65, 79–80, 81–82
Stabilization and Growth Act of *1967* (West Germany), 140
Standard industrial classification (SIC), 23, 69n
Steel industry, European, 9, 125–27
Stegamann, Klaus, 129n, 131n
Steiger, William, 96
Stolper, Wolfgang F., 17
Studebaker Corporation, 65, 79–82, 99, 151
SUB. *See* Supplemental unemployment benefits plan
Subsidies, 9–10, 136–37
Supplemental unemployment benefits (SUB) plan, 1, 3, 9, 109; adequacy of funds for, 80, 99; coverage of, 98; eligibility for, 98; fringe benefits and, 108
Supreme Court, 112
Sutton, Glenn, 48
Sweden: advance notice requirements, 102, 154; assistance for economic dislocation, 8; income maintenance programs, 141–42, 146; labor market programs, 141, 143 ; regional development program, 142
Swedish Investment Bank, 143

Tariff Commission: adjustment assistance petitions and, 41, 42, 43–44; delays in adjustment assistance findings by, 50–52; escape clause relief petitions and, 41, 42, 43; interpretation of adjustment assistance eligibility criteria, 47–49; membership of, 48–49; role in Automotive Products Act certification, 56, 57; rulings under Trade Expansion Act, 4, 45–47, 53, 59, 68
Tariffs, 1–2, 13
Tariff Schedule of the United States, 69n
Tax assistance, 1, 9; for German companies, 139; as incentive for private sector adjustment assistance, 155, 156; under Trade Expansion Act, 44, 64
Technical and Vocational Training Assistance Act of *1960* (Canada), 132
Technical assistance: to communities, 10, 75–76; to depressed areas, 87; extent of, 52; to firms, 9, 12, 64; purpose of, 44
Technological improvements, 110, 122; collective bargaining and, 101; in meat packing industry, 116; in railroad industry, 111; by scrapping obsolete equipment, 136
Textile and Clothing Board Act (Canada), 131
Textile Equipment and Other Temporary Measures Law (Japan), 145
Textile industry: aid for Canadian, 131; aid for Japanese, 9, 145, 146; aid for Sweden's, 143; aid for United Kingdom's, 9, 136, 137, 147; effect of imports on employment in, 28; productivity in, 30
Textile Workers Union of America, 101
Thunberg, Penelope, 48
Trade. *See* Foreign trade
Trade Act of *1974*, 1, 5–6, 19; benefits to communities, 66; benefits to firms, 64; benefits to workers, 63, 64–65, 67–68; efforts to improve benefit delivery under, 68; eligibility criteria, 60–61, 62, 67; evaluation of, 19, 150, 156–57; proposed improvements in, 71; provision for monitoring economic data, 68
Trade adjustment assistance: compensation principle and, 12–13, 19; deficiencies in, 20, 21; justification for, 10, 11, 12–13; proposed two-tier system for, 69–70; types of, 7–8; versus unemployment insurance, 96. *See also* Adjustment assistance, general; Automotive Products Trade Act of *1965*; Trade Act of *1974*; Trade Expansion Act of *1962*
Trade Agreements Act of *1934*, 1
Trade Agreements Act of *1951*, 2
Trade Expansion Act of *1962*: adjustment assistance provisions, 1–3, 39, 40–45, 61; adjustment assistance rul-

ings under, 46, 49; benefits to firms, 41, 42–43, 49–53; benefits to workers, 42, 53–55; eligibility criteria, 40, 41–44, 60; escape clause relief procedures, 40, 41, 43, 61; escape clause rulings, 45–46, 49; evaluation of, 19, 39, 57–58, 59, 150; expiration of, 49; Tariff Commission interpretation of, 47–49, 68

Transportation, Department of, 76

Truman, Harry S., 2

Unemployment: in Appalachia, 84, 86; in areas certified for adjustment assistance, 87; effect of manpower training programs on, 94; from elimination of obsolete equipment, 136–37; in meat packing industry, 117; from military base closings, 73, 75

Unemployment insurance, 9, 11; adequacy of, 151; benefits, 95, 99; in Canada, 132; coverage, 96; financing of, 96; proposed changes in, 153; severance pay and, 103; versus trade adjustment assistance, 96

United Automobile Workers, 3; employment services for South Bend, 81; negotiations over Chrysler plant closing, 153; SUB plan negotiated by, 98–99; support for liberal trade measures, 5

United Kingdom: aid to shipbuilding industry, 137–38; aid to textile industry, 9, 136, 137, 147; employment transfers in, 135; manpower programs, 134, 138, 146; readjustment assistance for industry, 136–38, 146; redundancy payments scheme, 135, 147, 155; regional development program, 134–35; required advance notice of employment termination, 102, 154; severance pay, 103

United Nations Conference on Trade and Development secretariat, 37

United Packinghouse, Food and Allied Workers, 117

United States Employment Service, 94

United States v. *Lowden*, 112n

Vocational Education Act of *1969* (West Germany), 140

Wage-employment guarantees, 99, 100

Wage equalization, 18, 20

Weber, Arnold R., 65n, 116n, 118n

Weinberg, Nat, 118n

Welfare programs: Japan, 147; U.S., 96–97, 151

West Germany: compensation for displaced workers, 125–26; employment services, 140; European Social Fund payments to, 128; regional development program, 139–40; tax incentives for business mergers, 139; trade adjustment assistance program, 139, 140, 141

Wichita, 76

Wilcock, Richard C., 65n, 118n

Wilcox, Clair, 2

Williams Commission Report, 2n

Workers: adjustment assistance benefits to, 42, 53–55, 63, 64–65, 67–68; adjustment assistance for older, 64–65, 153; advantage of two-tier adjustment assistance system for, 69–70; effect of adjustment assistance on, 8–9, 20; eligibility for assistance, 38, 40, 41–42, 60–61, 67; job search allowance for, 67, 147; productivity of, 28, 30, 33, 111; provision for interplant transfer of, 106–07. *See also* Collective bargaining; Displaced workers; Employment; Manpower training, foreign; Manpower training, U.S.; Relocation of workers; Unemployment

Work Incentive (WIN) program, 91, 92

Wright, Robert A., 81n

Young, Edwin, 118n

Young, J. Banks, 49